Whateverland

Whateverland
Learning to Live Here

Alexis Stewart and
Jennifer Koppelman Hutt

WILEY

John Wiley & Sons, Inc.

Design and composition by Forty-five Degree Design LLC

Designations used by companies to distinguish their products are often claimed as trademarks. In all instances where John Wiley & Sons, Inc., is aware of a claim, the product names appear in Initial Capital or ALL CAPITAL letters. Readers, however, should contact the appropriate companies for more complete information regarding trademarks and registration.

Published by John Wiley & Sons, Inc., Hoboken, New Jersey
Published simultaneously in Canada

For general information about our other products and services, please contact our Customer Care Department within the United States at (800) 762-2974, outside the United States at (317) 572-3993 or fax (317) 572-4002.

Wiley also publishes its books in a variety of electronic formats and by print-on-demand. Some content that appears in standard print versions of this book may not be available in other formats. For more information about Wiley products, visit us at www.wiley.com.

Library of Congress Cataloging-in-Publication Data:
Stewart, Alexis, date.
   Whateverland : learning to live here / Alexis Stewart and Jennifer Koppelman Hutt. —1st ed.
      p. cm.
   Includes index.
   ISBN 978-0-470-90758-0 (cloth; alk. paper); ISBN 978-1-118-10193-3 (ebk);
ISBN 978-1-118-10194-0 (ebk); ISBN 978-1-118-10195-7 (ebk)
 1. Life-skills—Handbooks, manuals, etc. I. Hutt, Jennifer Koppelman, 1970– II. Title.
   HQ2037.S74 2011
   646.70082—dc23
                                                                      2011026139

Printed in the United States of America

10 9 8 7 6 5 4 3 2 1

Thanks in advance to my mother for not getting angry about anything written in this book.

—*Alexis*

To Jacob and Raquel: You two are my reason for being. You're both really cute, and I love you like crazy.

To Keith: I know you don't love public displays of affection, but I love you and cherish you. And because you love all of me, I know I can accomplish anything I want to do. Thank you for picking up the slack for this very flawed working mother. I love you!

To my dad, Charles Koppelman: Thank you for everything. I love you.

To my mom, Bunny Koppelman: I miss you every single day. I hope you can read my book wherever you are. Love you.

—*Jennifer*

whatever |(h)wət-evər; (h)wät-|

1. *relative pronoun and adjective* used to emphasize a lack of restriction in referring to any thing or amount, no matter what.
2. *exclamation* used to express skepticism or exasperation.

—The New Oxford American Dictionary

what·ev·er [*hwuht*-EV-er]

1. Used in an argument to admit that you are wrong without admitting it so the argument is over. 2. Passive-aggressive behavior at its most eloquent. 3. A polite and less vulgar alternative to "Fuck You." 4. Uttered in a derisive and dismissive tone, in response to a confrontation or accusation which has been judged to be unimpressive, obnoxious, or disingenuous. Often used to dismiss someone when it is clear that rational discussion would be a waste of time and energy. 5. "I don't care." 6. Word used by Americans to connote a feeling of apathy.

—UrbanDictionary.com

Contents

Introduction

We're Not Qualified to Give Advice, but We Give It Anyway

You're not the only one who's crazy and full of shame. We are, too.

Alexis lightens the blow of her caustic personality by presenting new acquaintances with baked goods. While the rest of the world sleeps, Alexis bakes, cleans, or organizes, but she rarely consumes the fruits of her labor. In addition to being an insomniac, Alexis is obsessive about nutrition and exercise and, in the eyes of some people, pathologically oversexualized. So far, all of these issues have worked in her favor. She is highly productive, is superfit, and has never wanted for an orgasm.

Although *New York* magazine accused Alexis of being Martha's id, she is in reality much more than that: a voracious reader, a contentious cultural critic, and as much a devotee of Andy Rooney as of Andy Borowitz. Alexis has owned a series of businesses, all of which, unfortunately, eventually bored her. And although her mother's television show used to bore her as well, she really likes lampooning it with Jennifer.

For a long time Jennifer wouldn't look at her weight when she got on the scale—she paid a stranger to tell her whether she was down or up. Jennifer has a frighteningly comprehensive collection of Hello Kitty merchandise and an obsessive fear of flying. She is a self-congratulatory teetotaler who wears her emotions on her sleeve. When Jennifer doesn't hear from her husband for an hour, she worries that he's been hurt or incapacitated or that he's dead. She is an attorney, a notary, and a full-time mother of two children whose faces she won't allow to appear on the Internet.

Young Alexis.

Jenny with ringlets.

Jenny is brave enough to discuss her personal grief about losing her mother to pancreatic cancer in front of millions of people but is incapable of blow-drying her own hair (she can, however, rock a curling iron like the best of them).

Dolly Parton told Jennifer she'd be a star, Barbra Streisand was practically her aunt (Jennifer's father has been in the music business

Jennifer with her husband, Keith.

for fifty years), and she can sing and dance almost as well as many on Broadway. But Jennifer's best talent is her ability to connect with virtually anyone by using her charm, pathos, and self-deprecating humor. Everyone agrees that Jennifer would have been an excellent shrink, but who wants to deal with the proximity to blood and bodily fluids that medical school requires?

We've built careers on our neuroses. On our television and radio shows—*Whatever, Martha!*, *Whatever with Alexis and Jennifer*, and *Whatever, You're Wrong!*—we went on and on (and on) about our insecurities, our childhoods, our relationships, and our bathroom habits. With us, there's no such thing as TMI. Ever.

Alexis and Jennifer watching Martha while filming *Whatever, Martha!*

Even though technically we may not have been qualified to do so, we gave thoughtful, effective, just plain good advice to people every day, if we do say so ourselves. Between us we have an Ivy League degree, a law degree, a notary stamp, three children, one business, a hit radio show, and two phenomenal handbag collections—so that must count for something.

Why did we write this book, and why are you reading it? You're not the only one who needs help but hates self-help books.

We know that all of those other books tend to be written by established experts: industry leaders in the fields of organizational psychology, self-hypnosis, culinary mastery, home improvement, animal husbandry, or whatever. But we've yet to find one that is actually helpful. All they do is bring us face-to-face with our insecurities and inadequacies, presenting ridiculous solutions so bizarre they just lead to more problems. Craziest of all, they try to change people's fundamental natures, and that's just silly. People don't really change, after all. They just become more of who they really are.

So we set out to come up with a self-help book that would have lasting effects. And we couldn't think of a better way to make our suggestions last than to focus on the very things that people hate the most about themselves: their shameful behaviors, thoughts, feelings, failings, and insecurities. People's issues—including ours—are funny and so not unique.

Just to prove that we mean business and to let readers know that they're not alone, we've shared our own shameful behaviors, thoughts, feelings, failings, and insecurities. We're not afraid to be our own worst critics or to show our Achilles' heels. If we can thrive with our embarrassing, humiliating, shameful crap, then our readers can, too. Because you're only as sick as your secrets.

While Alexis is sarcastic, Jennifer is sincere. And when Alexis is sincere, Jennifer is—really, really surprised. Sometimes we agree, most of the time we don't, but we always have an opinion, and we never shut up. In other words, *this isn't your mother's self-help book.*

Portrait of Alexis.

And it's not Alexis's mother's self-help book, either. It's just two regular women (okay, who are we kidding, but whatever) talking about how coming to terms with who you really are—and who you're never going to be—isn't nearly as scary as you think.

1

What the Hell Is Homekeeping?

Alexis and Jennifer on Life at Home

In 1970, while I was living in New York City with my husband, Andy, and our young daughter, Alexis, we were told about a beautiful farmhouse for sale at 48 Turkey Hill Road South, in Westport, Connecticut. . . . Turkey Hill was a dream place for my family and me for many years. It taught us, it nurtured us, it fed us, and it occupied us in so many wonderful and instructive ways.

Martha Stewart

For the record, my mother has a cupboard with about seventy-eight scented candles in it. *Don't give her another one.* Just stop.

Alexis Stewart

I like to sleep next to my husband and a panic button that calls the police in case of emergency.

Jennifer Koppelman Hutt

7

J ennifer is a homebody (a euphemism, Alexis thinks, for *agoraphobe*), and Alexis has spent the past two years working on her giant apartment. Their living situations and tastes in interior design couldn't be more different: Alexis lives in the city and likes concrete, steel, and glass; Jennifer lives in the suburbs and likes pink and green. But they share a certain strong belief about their homes: no one—workmen, overnight guests, boyfriends, or even Martha—should be allowed in them for any extended period of time (and no more than absolutely necessary).

Hell Is Having Workmen in Your House (Unless You're Dating the Hot Contractor)

There are always workmen in my apartment. Workmen count on the fact that you're going to be *so* glad to see them go that you'll live with the mess they make and all of the bad, half-assed work they leave you with. I just want everyone to *get out*. I had one guy comment on what I was eating. I think his exact words were, "You're going to eat all of that?" And I said, "You're still here?" I've had workmen call for dates and leave me Halloween pumpkins. It never ends.

I only kind of liked one workman, but he didn't ask me out. He was married. And he was a chain smoker. But I dated a few contractors. Contractors are totally hot—because a contractor can make one phone call and get everything in your house fixed. It's unbelievable. And I continued to date them *way* past the point that I wanted to *just* because I wasn't sure if I could live without all of that help. I mean, one of them brought a scissor-lift into my house so I could clean all of my skylights from the inside. It was awesome! I kept *shtupping* him but as infrequently as possible.

Unfortunately, there's no way around it: you have to deal with repairs and upkeep. Things used to be built so well that Americans got away with never having to take care of things or they knew how to repair and maintain things themselves, but it's different now. Everything's built like crap. Keeping up with home repairs can be overwhelming and expensive, but let me tell you, keeping up with it is a hell of a lot cheaper than letting things go. Once you let things go, you're screwed.

If you don't know what you're supposed to do to keep your house from falling apart or falling down, you can do something really geeky, like follow Martha Stewart's Schedule for Home Maintenance, or you can try to realize the satisfaction you'll get out of figuring out how to fix something yourself. I think people underestimate how fun it is to learn how to do something yourself and get something accomplished—you'll get a little rush that you did it. And if you don't know how to do it, get a contractor. One without a plumber's crack. Although it depends on the crack.

—ALEXIS

I Didn't Like Sleepovers as a Kid, and I Don't Like Sleepovers Now

The best gift you can give your host is a hotel reservation for yourself. It's great to hang out all day. But I don't want sleepover dates with grown-ups. I didn't like them as a kid, and I don't like them now. I don't mean to be rude, but get out of my house. It doesn't make you a bad person if you hate houseguests. I'm a "people person," but I don't want you in my space for too long.

—JENNIFER

I Hate Houseguests

When someone calls and says, "I'm coming to New York!" I say, "Great! Where are you staying?" Once Martha asked if some of her friends could stay with me, and I said no. Then she got mad. I said, "I'd rather tape a one-thousand-dollar bill to my door for them than have them stay here." And she said, "Do they make one-thousand-dollar bills?" She missed the point. As usual.

Whenever I let someone stay, I'm always sorry. Once someone left all of the lights on. A half-eaten bagel and a half-empty coffee cup were on the counter, and a dirty dish was in the sink. I mean, *Are you kidding me? You can't turn off the lights?* I don't get it! This person never stayed over again. Shocking to say, it didn't affect the friendship.

Another time a friend of mine stayed with me in my mother's guesthouse, and I spent the whole time cleaning up around her. There were all these drinking glasses in her room, so I took them out, washed them, and put them away. Then she said, "I was keeping my contacts in there, but I won't be mad at you." Gee, thank you. Another person who stayed thought it would be funny, because I'm such a clean freak, to say things like "There's dust on that." When I apologized and cleaned it up, she said, "Oh, I'm only kidding!"

Jenny with braids.

Then there was the time some friends of mine stayed at my mother's house in Maine. This girl ended up crying because I wasn't spending enough time with her. Crying! She was the same girl who bit me at some point and then sent me a crazy e-mail!

—ALEXIS

The Only Thing Worse Than Having a Houseguest Is *Being* a Houseguest

I don't know which is worse, because I hate being a houseguest almost as much as I hate having houseguests. I end up cleaning my hosts' kitchens and closets. And it's always such a disappointment. One time I went to Jackson Hole, Wyoming. There was a blizzard, and after a fifteen-hour flight, I got there and my friend picked me up and showed me to *our* room and *our* bed. I was already dreading sharing a bathroom. Now we're sharing a *bed*?

She and her kids were staying in a condo, and I had to run around and open the curtains because there was no light. They'd already been there a week, and they hadn't let daylight into the house. *And* I'd sent a huge gift: champagne and cookies and a cake I'd baked—but they never even bothered to pick up the package from the post office even though I'd told them it was perishable and even though the post office was only a quarter of a mile away! I thought, Great. This is going to be fun.

—ALEXIS

I don't like being a houseguest, either. If I do sleep at your house, I'm a guest room kind of girl. I'm not into sharing a room—or a bed.

Also: Never. Ever. Drop. In. And calling from outside in the driveway doesn't constitute "notice." Sometimes when people

The Koppelman family home in the 1980s.

ring the doorbell unexpectedly, I choose not to answer the door. It's just inappropriate to show up unexpectedly. I might be having a moment of solitude. Or my husband and I could be having sex. I also hate when the phone rings at night—they'll call the home phone first and hang up when I don't answer (Hello-o-o-o?! Twenty-first century. Caller ID!), then they call the cell phone and leave a message, and then they call the home phone again so they can leave the message they didn't leave in the first place. Send an e-mail. Or send a text. People don't want to check their voice mail. If you want to talk, fine. But if you're just calling with a question, you can wait.

—JENNIFER

You're Not the Only One Who Doesn't Invite Martha Stewart Over for Dinner

My mother will occasionally complain that I don't invite her over for dinner, but can you blame me? Because sometimes this is what will happen: whatever I serve, she'll sip it, taste it, make a face, and then push it away. Then she'll disappear and start to clean up. She'll just get up from the table and I'll hear "What's this?" from the other room. You know me—I don't like other people touching my stuff. I'm an only child; it's *my* stuff.

—ALEXIS

Martha with baby Alexis in the kitchen.

The only thing worse than having workmen, houseguests, or Martha in your house is when the workmen use your bathroom—or when your boyfriend uses your bathroom. We know we're weirder and more neurotic about cleanliness and germs than most people reading this book—and it's an especially loaded topic for Jennifer, since she has so many bizarre bathroom issues to begin with (more about that later)—but that's what we're here to do: share our craziness so you feel less crazy!

I Hate When Workmen Use My Bathroom

One week I had two incidents with workmen using my bathroom. One was the cable guy; the other was an air-conditioning guy. Each spent an *unbelievable* amount of time in the bathroom. I was totally grossed out. There was pooping. It was disgusting! Fifteen minutes is a long time! I was pacing! I was so angry that they were pooping in my bathroom! It's irrational, sure, but still! You should find another place to do it—*not* in a customer's bathroom. One of them was going back and forth to the bathroom; he had some kind of stomach thing, clearly. And I felt bad for him—kind of—but please go elsewhere to do that sort of business!

—JENNIFER

I Hate When Boyfriends Use My Bathroom

I don't like when people have literature racks in their bathroom. On booty calls, I don't want to see magazines upside down on the floor. I don't want to know you go to the bathroom.

You're not human! I'm just having sex with you. We're not living together!

I also hate boyfriends who stay over and use all of the bathrooms. Use *one*. Pick *one*. And speaking of living with boyfriends and/or spouses: Separate houses. Separate bedrooms. Separate bathrooms. Like in the movie *Angels & Insects*.

I want privacy. Go. Away.

—ALEXIS

I Clogged Martha Stewart's Toilet

Everyone close to me (and now you) knows I have bathroom issues—that I can't poop anywhere but in my own bathroom. I was driving into the city one night to do the show, and I stopped on the way to get a cup of coffee. Shortly thereafter, I realized, OMG. I have to poop! When I absolutely have to poop somewhere that isn't my own home, I'm completely freaked out. So I was driving and driving and I was thinking, I'll be okay. I'll handle it, I'll do it, I'll get over it—I'll go at the studio because I have to. I don't have a choice.

By the time I got there I was completely desperate, so I went in there and figured it would be really fast because I really had to go, but as I was pooping I flushed the toilet so there wouldn't be any question of it all going down. Guess what happened? The toilet backed up! In midpoop! It wasn't even my fault! So the toilet filled with water, and I was in the bathroom, by myself, at Martha's studio, sweating and panicking, and I was thinking, OMG. I'm gonna have to go out there and call someone to help me. I didn't know what to do, so I started praying. To God. To anyone who would have me. I'm not even sure I'm a believer, but at that moment I had to do something to spare me the embarrassment of walking out there and getting help. Ultimately, the toilet did flush. God is great.

—JENNIFER

Alexis's Plungeless Cure for a Clogged Toilet

If you clog a toilet at someone's house, you just have to come out and be direct and say, "Um, we have a problem. I need a bucket." I devised a way to unclog a toilet without using a plunger, even if the people have a plunger in the bathroom, because I hate the splash-back. It's bad enough if it's your own poop or pee, but you really, really, *really* don't want someone else's poop or pee splashing in your face. So here's how you unclog a clogged toilet. The more water the better; it's all about the pressure and the temperature.

1. Fill a bucket (or a bowl or a plastic wastebasket) with hot water.
2. Fill the toilet to the brim with the hot water.
3. Walk away. It'll go down.

You're the Only One Whose Mother Doesn't Have a Key to Your Apartment Even Though She Owns It

I would go to camp, and while I was gone my mother would give away my jewelry because I didn't wear it. But if *I'd* given it away, she would have gone berserk. My stuff was her stuff, essentially. For as long as I can remember I have kept a "secret-free" house—you can't find anything in my house that would embarrass me. There's nothing to "find" in my house. And it's not that I've hidden it. There's just nothing to find. And there are some things that if you do find, you're the one who's going to be embarrassed—so go look.

The view from Alexis's Greenwich Village bedroom.

My mother doesn't have a key to my apartment even though she owns my apartment. Now, could she get in if she needed to? She panics about this! "What do you mean I don't get to have a key?"

Because you have no concept of what it means to want to have privacy! You don't want to have privacy! You want someone there every minute of every day, and I don't. I don't want to feel like I can be walked in on. And if that's the rule—if you own the apartment and you can walk in whenever you want—then I'll move. And never talk to you again! That'll be that. Either you're generous or you're not. There's no halfway. I don't want strings attached: here's an allowance—you're allowed to spend it only on what *I* want you to spend it on.

What? Then no. I don't want an allowance. Jennifer's family didn't have any interest in doing that to her. But maybe that's part of having three kids. You'd think my mother would have been too busy to be snooping around my crap, but obviously she wasn't.

—ALEXIS

Aside from bathroom issues, unwanted guests, and problematic mothers, here are some run-of-the-mill pet peeves, childhood baggage, and strange beliefs that clutter our homes and our minds.

Home Isn't Always Where the Heart Is

People always say, "Home is where the heart is." But the saying is actually "*If* home is where the heart is." It's from a poem. Everyone thinks it's a statement of fact, but it's not. Sometimes home isn't where the heart is. I know, it's deeply ironic coming from someone whose mother does what my mother does.

Maybe it has something to do with the fact that when I was six my parents moved from a beautiful apartment overlooking Riverside Drive and the Hudson River in Manhattan and dragged me to Connecticut, where I could play by myself in the dirt with no friends. We moved into this "charming" farmhouse with a bathtub but no shower (okay, there was a shower, but they chose not to fix it), and a Tupperware pitcher to wash your hair with. The cat would always poop in that particular bathroom as well. And there were no doorknobs. You stuck your finger in the hole and shut the door, and if you wanted the door to stay shut, you'd have to fold up a piece of paper and stick it in the door; that was how you kept the door closed.

My mother loves to tell everyone her favorite lines about the house: "The farmhouse at Turkey Hill was rundown and needed a lot of work. We had to learn how to do everything ourselves. Let's do it all ourselves! It's so much fun!" Here's what should have happened: That picture of the old house and the Mercedes? Bulldozer. We should have started from scratch. Everything would have been better. Even the Mercedes was a lemon!

Turkey Hill before the renovations.

Everyone always says, "But it was so beautiful!" Of course it looks beautiful in all the pictures! You think that comes with no torture? You think the pool cleans itself and the chickens feed themselves and the bricks lay themselves? Hardly. At the right time of day, everything looks good. What about in the heat of summer, when you're told to go weed for ten hours? Not so pretty anymore! Everybody looks at it through plateglass, sliding-door, air-conditioned, bug-free-environment eyes.

There were no sliding glass doors. We were lucky if there was a screen. You didn't stay inside. You went outside. *At all times.* And you weeded. And you laid brick. And you cleaned the chicken coop. "Just do it!" my mother would say. Nike should pay her royalties.

When you buy a house, your life is essentially over. You can't go anywhere, you're worried about everything all the time, and you'll never be able to enjoy a good hurricane again. I used to love storms, but not anymore. It's hard to enjoy a house, because you're always afraid people will wreck it if you have a party. So you can only have no-kids parties. Or stupid Christmas parties where everyone's so exhausted and tired already

Alexis and Martha in front of Turkey Hill.

they won't come or they won't do anything once they get there. Or parties with people who own houses themselves so they won't drop stuff on your rug.

People who don't own houses treat your house like a rental car. I had a party once with three hundred twentysomethings, and I was picking up shards of beer bottles and wine glasses from under the furniture for three years (no exaggeration). Now I live in a rather large apartment. I've been working on it for a while and have posted tons of photos on my blog: the construction, the moving in, the furniture, the unpacking, the book shelving, the medicine cabinets. People often comment on how long it's taken me—*years*—but I'm kind of a control freak. Gee, I wonder where I got that from.

—ALEXIS

My Mother Anthropomorphizes Textiles and Is Obsessed with Buckwheat Pillows

You're Probably the Only One Whose Mother Has Her Sheets Changed Every Day

Alexis: Martha always says she changes her sheets every day, but what she really means is that she *has* her sheets changed every day.

Jennifer: Every day? What is she, a bed wetter?

Martha believes that all clothes and linens must "breathe" at all times. These are her exact words: "They suffocate." I was never allowed to sit on my bed growing up because the quilt on it was an antique. When I was a kid, my mother put in her first book, "My daughter Alexis loves collecting old linens and lace." But it's not true. I can't stand collecting old linens and lace. I can appreciate old linens and lace, but I don't *want* old linens and lace.

My mother is obsessed with linens and bed making. She's also obsessed with those stupid buckwheat pillows. I hate those pillows. She's been pushing them on people for years, and they're the most annoying pillows on the planet. She gave me two of them when I got married. Let's just say that when my husband left, he didn't take them with him.

—ALEXIS

Antiquing with Martha

Alexis: I spent most of my childhood going antiquing with my mother, so I developed an appreciation for antiques. She even had an "antiquing kit"—a knife and a rope—to be "prepared" for transporting her finds home. It looked like a murder kit.

Jennifer: If I went antiquing with Martha and I saw something that we both wanted, who would go home with it?

Alexis: She would. No question.

Jennifer: Even if I, in fact, saw it first and pointed it out?

Alexis: Right. Not only that: the chances of you seeing it before she did? Highly unlikely. She can smell things. She just knows.

Keep Your Shoes On

You need to have the kind of house where you can leave your shoes on, otherwise what are the floors for? My mother has a sign on all of her doors to take your shoes off, but I walk right in and keep my shoes on. (Yes, mother, only if they're "clean.") I take my shoes off in my own house, too, but it's *requiring* the removal of your guests' shoes that bothers me, especially at a party, for God's sake! My mother's dogs piss and shit on her rugs. And she's telling people to take their shoes off?

—ALEXIS

No Natural Debris on the Property

At Skylands, my mother's house in Maine, there's no debris on the property at all. Nothing. I was there once with my dogs, and one of them pooped. I wanted to get a stick to spread the poop around so you couldn't see it—but no stick. Not a twig to be found. Someone's job is clearing off the entire property.

Then they collect the pine needles, put them in this thing that looks like a giant hamster wheel to clean them, and then they spread the clean pine needles all over the debris-free property.

—ALEXIS

The Safe Side of the Bed

I have to sleep on the safe side of the bed. That's the side farthest away from the door, so you're protected if someone breaks in.

—JENNIFER

Alexis and Jennifer's Home Decor Rules

1. *Art is overrated.* You can't afford the crap you want, so you buy some other crap and you get bored with it. I'm sorry, but you can't really get bored with your blank wall. Or your books that change all the time and that have some meaning instead of some mediocre painting that you bought because you only had $300.

2. *Don't get a piano.* Unless you actually can play. We hate the look of a piano. It's just another thing to dust. And it'll never be in tune. Then you have to have another standing appointment for home maintenance, like having your chandelier cleaned.

3. *Don't get a chandelier you can't clean yourself.* Or that doesn't have a switch to lower it like the one in one of Jennifer's favorite movies, *Working Girl*.

4. *Don't fill your garage with all of your crap.* Garages are for cars. We know so many people who don't use their garages for anything except crap. They have treadmills. They have extra refrigerators, an extra freezer (which is fine if it works

and if you *leave room* for the car). They have all sorts of equipment. It's your garage, not your basement. You don't want it to get too comfortable, because you're going to be living out there soon. So don't make it too inviting. It's not for your futon. It's for your car. And it's also not for your weight rack. Go to a gym. First of all, you're not going to use a treadmill in your garage. It's miserable, it's damp, it's nasty. It's not going to work, so don't put it in there—invest in a gym membership and go. If you don't have a nice place for the treadmill, don't get one. And if you don't have a TV in front of your treadmill, you're fooling yourself. You can't just stare at a wall or listen to music.

5. *If you want your house to look bigger, paint everything—walls and ceilings—the same color.* Your house will look much bigger than it is. If you start detailing, it looks smaller. Choose a color. Get those pint paint cans and tape off a square on your wall. If you're not sure which color you like, do a couple of colors in a couple of rooms. Check them out in daylight and at night. Or if you're going to do the whole house, try the colors on a couple of different walls so you can see what they look like in different light. Or you could paint one wall a weird color instead of painting the whole room orange, which might drive you insane.

6. *Have uniform bathrooms throughout the house.* There's something soothing and nice about everything being the same.

7. *A bare bulb is not okay.* Lighting is hard, because nobody makes a good lamp, but a bare bulb is not okay. Go out and get yourself a Chinese paper lantern. They're cute, and they come in all shapes, colors, and sizes. A three-dollar Chinese lantern will make your bedroom look cute, or you could put up several lanterns at different heights. You have to get a multispectrum bulb: the lighting from those new fluorescent bulbs is just horrible. Overhead lighting is very difficult to get right—lamps are much better, except in the kitchen. But in

almost any other room, especially the dining room, you want something over the table, but it's rough. That lighting over your head—nobody looks good. And you need to invest in dimmers.

8. *An easy fix if your house is really dusty and you can't deal with it: pull down the shades so you won't see it.* If you have a dusty house and it makes you insane, close the blinds.

9. *Put EZ-Glides under your furniture.* It makes moving things easier, and it protects your floors.

2

Does Talking to Pop-Tarts Mean You're Crazy?

Alexis and Jennifer on Food and Eating

When Martha eats baked beans out of a can, her favorite part is the cube of fat.

Alexis Stewart

My mother knew that people preferred to eat chocolate alone somewhere. In secret. That's why in our house she'd keep chocolate in a little bowl on the bathroom sink, as if they were guest soap.

Jennifer Koppelman Hutt

Have as many as you like. One is fine.
Martha Stewart, to children eating freshly baked
cookies on her show

⁓

Alexis hasn't eaten meat since I fed her Plantagenet Palliser.
Martha Stewart

To eat crap or not to eat crap: that's another topic—food—on which Alexis and Jennifer often differ.

Alexis grew up on lemon sorbet and sunny fish (whatever sunny fish is), while Jennifer became a *connoisseuse* of Pop-Tarts and pizza.

Jennifer has recently radically changed her eating habits, but she still craves junk food. Alexis craves junk food, too—to her, junk food includes frozen peas and anything in a package.

If we could, we'd insert a little picture of Jennifer rolling her eyes right now and mouthing the word *freak* because really, who else but Alexis would consider frozen vegetables to be junk food? But that's what we're dealing with here: a radically bizarre childhood in which there wasn't any prepackaged store-bought food in the house. Sometimes there wasn't *any* food in Alexis's house, but that's another story (keep reading). In the meantime, Alexis and Jennifer compare notes on what they ate, what they hate, and family *mishigas* around eating and food.

I Let Alexis Clean Out My Refrigerator and Cabinets

Alexis likes to spread her knowledge of good eating and staying healthy. Three weeks after we met, she came to my house and was like "Your kids can't have this! Oh no! They can't have that! What's wrong with you?" She cleared out my whole kitchen, threw out all the partially hydrogenated oil–containing and high fructose corn syrup–containing stuff. So we were left with very little. She said she'd never seen so much junk food in her life—that it was a junk-food paradise because there was candy on the counter all the time. Before meeting Alexis six years ago, I didn't think about high fructose corn syrup because I didn't know about it. Now I know I can buy yogurt that's healthy and organic—you know, the kind that doesn't have Trix or Oreos on top to mix in.

—JENNIFER

Crappy Food

I don't eat shitty food. I won't. I don't understand it. People are so used to eating being an immediate gratification that they don't realize that they will like or can learn to like—and even to love and to learn to crave—things that aren't bad for them.

Alexis bobbing
for apples.

It just takes a little practice. It's the only body you've got. So if you eat badly and ruin your body, that's it. It's over! Do you really want to mess with it? Because then you're dead.

—ALEXIS

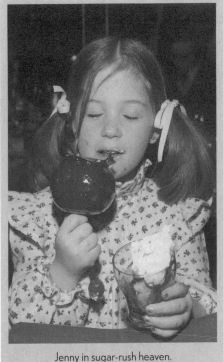

Jenny in sugar-rush heaven.

I Talk to Pop-Tarts

I've been known to talk to food and say, "I'll see you again. I'm not going to have you today, but I'll have you another day." I was in the supermarket the other day—I must have looked like the biggest asshole. I stood in front of the Pop-Tarts for five full minutes. I got completely confused and drawn in. I didn't buy any, but I stared at every flavor and analyzed them and talked to myself like a loser. "I like the strawberry. I don't like the milkshake flavor. I don't like the ice cream sundae flavor. I don't like the chocolate chip flavor. I do like the blueberry flavor."

I know what they all taste like. I had a full conversation with myself as I looked at them. Then I stepped away from the Pop-Tarts, talked to myself, and walked away. But I was there for just a few minutes too long. It was embarrassing. The store manager saw me. I was mortified.

—JENNIFER

True Confessions: I Grew Up Craving Frozen Peas and Packaged Food

I love healthy food. I just do—probably because I was raised with such natural, good food. But throughout my entire childhood I would run over to my friend's house for her Strawberry Quik, Cheez Doodles, and Oreos. Sometimes I would drink a little cup of heavy cream with sugar in it, because there was nothing else. That was the only thing! My mother cooked real dinners, and all I wanted was packaged food. I wanted my parents to go away so I could have things like boil-in-the-bag peas and those frozen turkey TV dinners. To me, packaged food was junk food. There was butter on it. Junk food to me is anything you're not supposed to have.

—ALEXIS

Growing Up, Food Was Love

In my house, food was weird. There was lots of junk, and tons and tons of baked goods for my mother that I wasn't supposed to eat, but I ate them anyway. I don't know why she felt like she needed to have so much baked stuff around, but it was probably because her mother didn't give her attention and withheld all emotional contact, even food. It goes to the whole food-is-love thing. Her mother was very strange; it was all about appearance. My mother was into appearance, too, but she was also very lovey-dovey, so I'm still not sure why I needed so much food.

—JENNIFER

Growing Up, Food Was Not Love

Food was not love in my house. Not at all. Food was just food—assuming there was any in the house.

—ALEXIS

Ice Cream Cones and Dr. Ruth Westheimer

Alexis: I don't like the ice cream cone. I like the cup. I don't like watching people lick the cone. I don't like the dripping down the cone. It's gross.

Jennifer: There's a trick to a cone. When I was a kid, on Sunday nights, I would listen to Dr. Ruth Westheimer on the radio. Someone called in to talk about oral sex and she said, "Just pretend it's an ice cream cone." That kind of stuck with me.

Alexis: Because you like ice cream.

Jennifer: Yes. Because I like "ice cream."

Alexis is not amused by her food.

You're Not the Only One Whose Mother Fed You One of the Family Farm Animals

My mother attributes my vegetarianism to the time she served me Plantagenet Palliser.

It was our lamb. My mother took great glee in telling me midmeal, "Do you know where this came from? Do you like it?"

—ALEXIS

Takeout, Fake Cheese, and "Chicken Fingers"

I don't eat fast food. I don't eat prepared food. I hate takeout and getting takeout delivered to your house. I don't understand it. It doesn't taste good. It's gross! Why can't you just scramble some eggs or throw some pasta in a pot? I don't get it. It's expensive, and it doesn't taste like it tastes in the restaurant. The portions are never the same, and it costs twice as much. There was a family in the building I used to live in, and they had delivery every night for dinner. *Every single night.* I just don't understand it. I don't know what's wrong with them.

I don't eat American Chinese food. If I knew where really good Indian food was, I might eat that. I don't like shitty food. So I might be a food snob, but I can eat really simple food. I'm fine with a plate of spaghetti with a little cheese and tomatoes on it. But I don't want garbage. I'm not interested. And as often as possible I try to make my own lunch and take it to work with me.

I love cheese. But the cheese most people eat now isn't even real cheese. And God forbid you eat a vegetable that isn't bathed or smothered in "cheese." I don't understand it. People have different attitudes about how they want to consume their calories. A piece of cheese? Okay. But I don't want *cheese soup*. Cheese soup is the most incomprehensible food there is. And Welsh Rabbit. Or Rarebit. Whatever that stuff is called. Can I just have some good bread with cheese? Why do I have to have this slop? I love fondue, but it has to be good fondue. It can't be funky fondue. And it has to be on your birthday.

What is this goddamn obsession with chicken fingers? When I was growing up, there were no chicken fingers. There were chicken *legs*. My mother certainly did not make me chicken fingers when I was little. She barely remembered to feed me, she was so busy with her catering business. I mean, now she has a recipe for easy healthy chicken fingers—oh great!—but she certainly didn't then.

—ALEXIS

Jennifer Knows the Number of Calories in Everything

One of Jennifer's bizarre talents is figuring out the exact caloric value of a slice of anything. I think it's much more fattening if you know the calories. I don't know the calories in anything.

—ALEXIS

Jennifer loves chicken fingers, by the way. Now that the chicken finger issue has been raised, an issue that triggers in Alexis a volcanic rage about how children today eat—terribly, stupidly, unhealthily—it's time to talk about some of her other favorite hot-button topics: the decline of Western civilization with the invention of children's menus, the proliferation of chicken fingers and the disappearance of real chicken parts (like chicken legs), and the fact that as a nation, we've created a generation of food separatists—children who don't eat what their parents eat and require infantilized versions of grown-ups' food. In the World According to Alexis, kids can learn to like anything—if only their parents expose them to it early enough in life.

Alexis's Rules for Kids and Food

When children are babies, you can completely control their food choices, so the excuse that they like something or they don't like something else, when they don't know the difference, is completely irritating to me. Just because it's easier for you to grab a Popsicle and stick it in your one-year-old's mouth doesn't mean you should. Kids don't have to taste a Popsicle until the day they grab one from some other kid—it's ridiculous. You have complete and utter control. You could feed them blubber and they'd like it: if they got hungry, they'd learn to like it. You think Eskimo kids say, "I don't feel like blubber! Get me a sandwich!" When your kid doesn't know what food is, you decide for him.

I also don't understand why children have to eat differently from adults. I didn't. There's *no* reason for it. Why do people have to order off the children's menu? Why can't they order off the regular menu and take the rest home? Everything can be kid-friendly. Everything! People aren't usually eating caviar. I'm pretty sure that almost every item on a children's menu, including all packaged food, is less healthy than regular adult food. "Kid food" is full of fat and sugar and starch and salt.

I don't get it. Kids want to be grown-ups, so why don't they want to eat adult food? Parents have the power to get their kids to taste different foods, and you can decide if you're going to be lazy about it or not. It doesn't have anything to do with money.

You can teach kids how to cook so they understand food. And just moving and standing up and doing something instead of sitting helps. Then they know where food comes from and how it's made. Food shouldn't be the reward for everything, and every screaming child shouldn't get candy shoved in her face. If you go get ice cream, it shouldn't be "If you do this, you get ice cream." It should be "Yay! We're going to the movies, and then we're getting ice cream." How about "You do this, and then on other days we'll do fun things?" No ice cream bribe necessary.

~

Now it's Jennifer's turn. You'll notice a less strident tone. A certain lack of rage.

Jennifer's Rules for Eating

I always have a little bit of candy in my bag or a little bit of chocolate—a lollipop or something. I like to know I have it even if I don't eat it. Often I give it out—I'll hand out four Rollos. There's still such shame in buying candy when you want it. My mother knew that people preferred to eat chocolate alone somewhere. In secret. That's why in her house she'd keep chocolate in a little bowl on the bathroom sink, like guest soap.

During my sophomore year of college, this girl I knew went home for Christmas vacation and came back to school doing the Optifast diet—a liquid diet popular in the eighties. Between January and March she got really skinny, so I decided I wanted to try it, too. She invited me to her family's house in Steamboat Springs, Colorado, for spring break, and I had just started the diet. She was wearing these superskinny ski pants. I was wearing one of those big toddler-style purple ski suits, and I was *dying*. I'd only had a vanilla powdered shake, and I'm not great at fasting, so I snuck some M&Ms with me, but even that didn't help. I was starving. Anyway, after a full day of skiing, we had dinner—Domino's Pizza—and by *we*, I mean everyone else had pizza and I had a shake.

Then everyone went to bed. Except me. I was still hungry, and I was dreaming of pizza—the half-pizza that was left over because they had eaten only half of that pizza because they're normal people. The next day, everyone went skiing again, and by midday I went back to watch TV. I was sitting there, and I thought, Don't do it. But I couldn't help it. I finished the half-pizza that was in the refrigerator, then I called Domino's and ordered a whole new pizza, then I ate half of that so that I could replace the half I'd eaten with the new half I hadn't eaten. Then I threw away the new box and put the new half-pizza in the old box and put it back in the refrigerator. And nobody ever found out. I'm surprised nobody questioned why the Optifast diet didn't work for me.

I don't like when people bully other people about what they're eating or what they're choosing to eat. I'm not talking about unhealthy versus healthy—I'm not saying if you're eating a tub of Crisco—food styles is what I'm referring to. If you choose to eat at four o'clock and not eight o'clock, and then you go out to dinner with someone and you've already eaten, so you just want to have tea or you just want to have lettuce, that should be okay. If you're going out to be social, or you don't like where you're going or whatever it is, I don't think you should have to eat if you don't feel like eating.

Don't Go Out to Dinner, Not Eat Anything, and Lie about Why You're Not Eating Anything

I think it's annoying to go out to dinner and not eat. Plan your schedule. If you're going out to dinner, plan on eating dinner there. And if you're not going to eat, then be honest about it.

Say, "I used to be fat and now I'm afraid to eat anything." Most people aren't honest. They say, "Oh, I'm *so* full" or "I'm allergic to everything in this restaurant!" Just say, "I'm afraid of gaining weight, so I'm just going to have some soda water and watch you eat. I hope that doesn't make you uncomfortable."

—ALEXIS

Enough with the intense food issues! Here's where we share more weird and funny food issues.

Chutney Is the Great Cosmic Joke

I always clean or organize something when I'm at my mother's. I'll be cleaning out the "tea drawer" or the "chocolate drawer" or the "condiments cabinet." Usually it's because she's asked me to do something else much worse, so I'll focus on a drawer that *really* needs editing. And I'll find an old jar of chutney. I'll ask her if I can throw it away, and she'll say no, "I'll use it on a hot dog." Like when was the last time she ate a hot dog (at home)? Giving chutney as a gift is ridiculous. It's the great cosmic joke. Americans don't eat chutney! It's not our condiment. It's a mystery! No one knows what to do with it, unless maybe you're in an Indian restaurant and you want to believe that if you eat some it'll help make the really hot thing you just ate go away. And it's always in an ugly jar with a plaid top or a piece of fabric and a bow and a rubber band around it. It's just gross and totally unacceptable.

—ALEXIS

Christmas Eve at Martha's

Christmas Eve Menu from Martha's Maine House

Lobster Newburg

Fresh Bean Hash

Twice-Baked Potatoes Stuffed with Spinach and Parsnip Soufflés

Endive Petals with Smoked Scallops

Shrimp Salad Rolls

Finnan Haddie Canapés

Creamy Red and Green Cabbage

Roasted Rack of Venison with Red-Currant-and-Cranberry Sauce

Lardy Cake

Torie's Chocolate-Chunk Toffee Cookies

Chocolate-Applesauce Cake

Cider Glaze, Apple Chips, and Crystallized Ginger

Christmas Menu from Martha's East Hampton House

Oysters with Festive Mignonette

Prime Rib

Yorkshire Pudding

Baked Quince with Onions, Wild Mushrooms, and Madeira Glaze

Brussels Sprouts Puree

Gingerbread Trifle with Cognac Custard and Pears

Steamed Pudding with Kumquat Marmalade

Ginger Baba au Rhum

Potlucks Are an Abomination

Potlucks are an outrage. I don't know what I'm getting. Who wants a potluck meal, anyway? You have no idea what you're in for. Plus, not everybody can cook. And don't invite me for dinner at seven and then not sit down to eat until nine-thirty. I'm not emotionally prepared for that. I have to get up early the next day, and now I'm going to watch you cook or have to help you cook? If that's the plan, great. But please don't surprise me.

—ALEXIS

I Hate Holiday Food

I hate holiday food. It's so exhausting, and everyone makes too much. I like cookies because they're pretty. I like making them pretty or making a display, but holiday food is boring to me because typically it's food that I don't want to eat, and just because it's a holiday doesn't make me want to eat it. I don't eat meat, so that nixes just about everything. And if I do sneak some of the stuffing that somebody pretended was vegetarian, then I'll just be burping for the next four days. I don't like marshmallows on my sweet potatoes. I don't like pumpkin pie. Garrison Keillor said that pumpkin pie was the ultimate symbol of mediocrity because the best pumpkin pie you've ever had isn't that different from the worst pumpkin pie you've ever had.

—ALEXIS

Our Jewish Holiday Meals

I always liked my mother's noodle pudding. So that to me was a holiday food I liked. Every holiday was like Thanksgiving in my house—it was pretty much the same meal. Except that at Passover, instead of bread there was matzo. It was like Thanksgiving with matzo.

—JENNIFER

My Mother Always Stole the Best Part of My Croissants

My mother used to make *the* best croissants. Her croissants were amazing, and the outside was my favorite part. The crunchy crusty outside. I'd eat the inside first because that *wasn't* my favorite part, and I'd save the outside for last, but then I'd turn around for one second and it would be gone. I'd look at my mother and ask, "What happened?" and she'd say, "Oh, I thought you didn't want it." She'd swipe it every time.

—ALEXIS

My Jewish Mother's Favorite Sandwich

Whenever my mother would order a ham sandwich, she'd pretend it was for someone else. She'd say, "Virginia ham, cheddar cheese, and extra mayo—*because she likes it that way.*"

—JENNIFER

I'm a Vegetarian Who Wears Leather

When I was a kid, as soon as I heard about the rain forest being cut down for cows, that was it for me. I didn't need meat that badly. But if anyone wants to argue with me about this, they can. *Leather is a by-product.* When they stop killing cows, I'll stop wearing leather.

—ALEXIS

Here's another thing we agree on: cutting back on sweets so your teeth don't fall out like a drug addict's. It's hard, because most of us are addicted to sugar—and chocolate—and everything else sweet. Wondering what to do about it? You've come to the right place.

Alexis and Jennifer's Advice for Cutting Back on Sugar

Are you a toothbrush away from looking like a crystal meth addict? Most people we know are addicted to sugar. Of course, we can totally relate. Sugar Daddies, Sugar Babies, Sour Patch Kids—sugar is delicious! Not to mention baked goods. And all things chocolate. Sure, it's fattening, but being addicted to sugar is way better than being addicted to meth. So congratulations! It's much less obnoxious than being an annoying carbophobe.

But even though eating too much sugar is better than being a drug addict, it's still not a good thing. Not only does it make you fat and ruin your teeth, it really messes with your body's insulin response, which screws up all of your internal systems. You could try a no sugar, no flour diet, which will definitely make you feel better, but it's really, really hard. Whatever you do, don't try the

Atkins diet: it made Jennifer feel sicker than she's ever felt in her entire life. Instead of getting crazy and doing something drastic, try watching your refined carbohydrates and focus on fruits, vegetables, protein, and whole grains. Proteins, fats, fruits, vegetables, and whole grains don't produce the insulin response sugar does.

Here are some things to try if you're addicted to sugar and no longer want to be:

- *Wrap up all of the sweet stuff in your house and give your friends and coworkers spontaneous presents.* This will earn you brownie (and cookie and cake) points as well as eliminate temptation.

- *Give up fake sweeteners.* This sounds counterintuitive, but it works—even though they don't contain sugar, we think Splenda, Sweet 'N Low, and Equal increase cravings, the same way having a "harmless" little taste of frosting can lead to you gulping down the whole bowl. Not to mention the fact that they're toxic. There have been studies showing that people who drink diet soda weigh more on average than people who drink regular soda. The skinniest people, of course, drink no soda at all.

- *Follow Alexis's Baking Plan:* This strategy may be controversial, but I swear by it: bake obsessively. But don't eat what you bake. I like baking because it's creative, and giving it away means I don't have to eat it. I don't give it to people who are trying to lose weight (although I used to give a male friend of my mother's extra large pieces of chocolate cake with chocolate frosting, hoping he would have a heart attack right there in front of me). Also, if you never put your batter-covered finger in your mouth, you won't finish half of the raw cookie dough before you have a chance to bake it.

- *Have cheese or sorbet without cookies for dessert instead of cake.* Have your coffee without sugar (soon you won't miss it). The Europeans have been doing it forever, and they're much thinner than we are.

The Alexis Cleanse

Finding a new guy or breaking up with one you like will always help to keep your weight down. I actually look forward to dramatic and stressful shifts like this, because at least I'll come through them looking fantastic. Short of a traumatic breakup or meeting a hot new sexual partner, this is how I recommend you stay fit:

- Wake up and drink a giant bottle of water.

- Exercise for four hours.

- Eat a block of tofu with Frank's Red Hot sauce and drink the sauce. The sodium will keep you from becoming dehydrated.

- Drink some green tea to keep you awake despite your low caloric intake. A bonus: green tea speeds up your metabolism.

- Walk up and down the subway stairs to and from work in six-inch platform heels and really tight jeans that constantly remind you of how fat you are.

- Drink a bottle and a half of wine and eat a hunk of parmigiano reggiano cheese (protein!).

- *Shtup* a New Guy or pass out.

- Repeat.

The Jennifer Cleanse

Drink a cup of coffee however you like it: with sugar and cream or without either. There's something liberating about allowing yourself to have coffee exactly the way you want it each day without judgment. Then do this:

- Eat no breakfast except what your kids leave on their plates.

- Eat no lunch except what your kids leave on their plates.

- Eat no dinner except what your kids leave on their plates.

- Watch mind-numbing reality TV in order to distract yourself from the sensation of starving.

- Go to bed early. Really early.

- Repeat.

Just because Alexis grew up with healthy eating habits doesn't mean that everyone else did. Jennifer certainly didn't, and because of that she's waged a lifelong battle with food. Last year, the war became a holy one, and her jihad to get control of her eating and her body began. A year later, she's much smaller and much healthier. Here's how she got from there to here.

Jennifer's Weight-Loss Story

When I was growing up, my mother tortured me about my weight. She wasn't a waif, and she never felt good about her body, but she had complete control over what she did and didn't consume. Because of that, she was ultimately, after many years of trying, superthin. So I suppose my lack of control or my inability to be as controlled as she was with food made her crazy—more, I believe, because she wanted to save me from the pain of being fat than for any other reason. Maybe my mom's intense desire for me to be thin made my actually getting thin that much harder. I couldn't be thin and give my mother what she wanted (even if it meant giving *me* what I wanted, too).

I know now that her intentions were only good. As a mother myself, I totally get the need to protect your child from pain, but my mother's delivery of that message was wacky, and

I suffered a lot because of it. I spent most of my life wondering why my worth was contingent on the number on the scale. I knew that in every other way my mother loved me intensely—and lived for me—and that in her core she wanted nothing more than to be with me and provide me with a happy-go-lucky carefree life and make me feel loved. That said, my weight enraged her. And as well as she could control her food intake, she couldn't control that rage.

I believe mothers become mothers with the same issues they had before they were mothers, and I suppose my mom's own body issues made it very tough for her to teach me how to love and nurture my own body in a healthy way. Growing up, and well into my adulthood, I didn't feel good about my body. When I was a child, my overweightness fluctuated within a pretty normal range—more fat some years, less fat others—but I was always a little bit fat. I was plenty cute without knowing it, had lots of friends, and liked some boys who liked me back and many who did not, but I blamed every moment of sadness and failure on my not being built like a ballerina. Even though the rational part of me today knows how nutty that mentality was, that mind-set stayed with me for a long, long time.

When I graduated from college, I came home fat—not as fat as I was in recent years, but fat nonetheless. The minute I got home it was understood that I'd spend that summer getting thin—this was of the utmost importance, because my sister was getting married, and there was *no way* I was going to be a fat maid of honor. So my parents got me a personal trainer, and I exercised every day for hours and lost twenty-five pounds in ten weeks. I was twenty-two years old, and I finally looked good.

But even though I had a hot body, I had no idea that I did. I was nervous and insecure, and I didn't feel at all like my problems were now solved by being thin. In fact, I was a complete basket case. I would wake up in the morning and get on the scale, then I would pee and get on the scale, then I would poop and get on the scale, then I'd eat something or exercise or drink something and get on the scale. All day it was like this—on the scale and off the scale—and every mood was determined by that number on the scale.

Before I lost weight, I believed that being thin meant no more boy troubles, but while I was thin the boy I loved said he loved me back but promptly "loved" someone else at the same time, and we broke up. I exercised a lot to get over the pain of that breakup, until I jumped in an aerobics class and landed poorly and tore a ligament in my leg. Two days later the scale read five pounds heavier, and that's when I gave up the scale.

The next three years are a blur, weightwise, because I didn't get on a scale at all. I'm certain my weight must have fluctuated twenty pounds, but the next time I did get on the scale I was not happy with the number I saw. I wasn't obese, technically. I was just fat. I started dieting, and even though I didn't lose all that much weight, I lost enough to feel better.

I met my husband during this time. I was twenty-five, and he loved my body just the way it was. He thought my body was hot, even though I didn't, and he nourished me in a way that made me not need food. Ha. Kidding. I wish! I ate with my then fiancé, now husband—too much—and gained weight. But I also laughed and lived and felt happy. Because I was getting married to a wonderful man, my mother wasn't as obsessed with my body, and, amazingly enough, I got married at a not-thin weight.

I had two children pretty quickly, and I wound up clinically obese after each of them was born. I didn't do enough to deal with it, and although I cared about what I looked like, I didn't really want to see what I looked like. For me, the reflection in the mirror was always fatter than I felt—by which I mean that even though I felt really fat, the reflection staring back at me and the photographs I saw of myself were always way worse than what I expected to see. I exercised and I dieted, but I did both without intensity or determination, so I didn't see results.

One Way to Watch Your Weight

My mother used to say, "Taste it and waste it." It's not very green, but it's certainly a method of calorie restriction.

—JENNIFER

Then, when I was thirty-five, I started working, and suddenly everything changed for me. My mother was getting to know me from a different perspective (she was a daily listener of our radio show from day one), and she was so proud of me, so not focused on my body and my weight, that my self-worth seemed to triple. Soon after that, I started to take better care of myself and move in a more positive direction, weightwise.

Then my mother got sick, and then she died, and after I lost her I blew up like a balloon.

It took a while for me to deal with that loss and the resulting weight gain—to deal with it in an "I'm going to lose my life if I don't" kind of way—and now, a year and a half after I started, I've lost over sixty-five pounds. People can't believe how quickly I've lost weight, when, in reality, it has taken me a long time. I haven't lost more than six pounds in any one month.

The irony of my mother being dead and my finally being thin is not lost on me at all. It makes me sad sometimes, though, knowing that she would have derived so much pleasure from seeing me now, thin and healthy. And I don't know how to respond to the people who haven't seen me in months and comment on my weight loss. If I just say, "Thank you," am I an asshole? If I respond with "I feel terrific!" is that bragging? People say to me, "I didn't recognize you!" or "You're a different person!" or "You must be so happy!" or "You were so fat!" (yup, people actually say that!)—and now I feel like I'm part of this club where the antifat people can be open around me and express their disgust for overweight people since I won't be offended because I'm not overweight anymore.

But once a fatty, always a fatty.

Don't get me wrong: I appreciate the compliments. It's validating and amazingly cool to be referred to as "tiny" or a "peanut" or "pretty." Those are words that weren't used to describe me for many years—someone even called me hot—and even though I'm way out of my comfort zone sometimes, I'm learning to accept these compliments and let them wash over me. I've worked hard and am still working hard. It should be okay for me to admit that and accept the positive feedback.

But the other side of these compliments is the knowledge that many people are just waiting for me to gain it all back. Statistically, most people do gain their weight back, and I don't want to be one of those statistics. I'm so afraid of gaining it back that when someone asks me if I want to lose more or what my plan is, the only thing I can think of is that I have to do anything I can not to get fat again.

People always ask me how I did it—what plan I followed. I don't follow any one program, although I'm a huge fan of Weight Watchers. My food choices are random but always mindful—meaning that I might eat candy, but I count all the calories and just have a little, or I'll counter it by having a healthy salad. My exercise is always at least one hour—often more—almost every day. And I weigh myself almost every morning. I don't see myself as a weight-loss success story. Five years from now, when I'm (God willing) still this size, I'll shout my success from the rooftops. And even though I know I'll always struggle and work hard to do right by my body, I feel great about where I am now: forty years old and thin, with a belly in need of a tummy tuck that I am *so* not ready to get.

- You can start again at every meal. If you screw up breakfast, do better at lunch.

- It's not insane to talk to yourself or to your food. "Hey, pizza, I really want to eat you, but I'm going to choose to not eat you today. You'll be there when I really need to have you!"

- Any movement is better than no movement. Exercise can be anything you want it to be. If you hate the treadmill, do the elliptical. If you hate machines, take a walk or a dance class, or just put on music and dance by yourself for thirty minutes or an hour.

**Jennifer's
Diet and
Exercise Rules**

- Again, you can always start over.
- Throw away your fat clothes. Scary, but it must be done.
- If you like to be with people, get friends to exercise with you.
- If not, do it alone!
- Start with small goals. After a while, all of those small goals reached will equal reaching a big goal.
- Don't forget: you can always start over!

Stop Eating One Thing That's Bad for You

My favorite eating tip is this: take one thing that's bad for you that you eat every day—one of those things—and stop eating it for two weeks and see what happens. Or do it for a week. It's only a week. And then you can have it again. What'll probably happen is that by the end of the week you won't need to have it again. You won't want it. You won't care.

—ALEXIS

Just Keep Trying

Secret Recipes

Jennifer: Why does Martha always try to get someone's secret recipe?

Alexis: I think because it's so annoying to her that it's a secret.

This is a great mantra: It's the only body you have. So be mindful. Because even if you're not as vigilant about your food choices as Alexis is, everyone should eat fewer processed foods and switch to organic animal protein. It doesn't mean that you can never have a potato chip. Food is sustenance and food is fuel, but food is also pleasure. You should be able to enjoy what you're eating when you're eating it. You don't have to make drastic changes. It might mean that you keep trying to eat healthier, that you keep trying to take better care of yourself. It's not about beating yourself up because you haven't accomplished what you want to accomplish. It's about constantly trying to do better for the one body that you have. Make small changes. For example, if you're somebody who eats red meat four days a week, knock it down to two.

—JENNIFER

Alexis gets the last word here so that her message to eat clean and healthy stays with you.

Eat Clean Food

If you're not buying chicken from one of approximately three places on the planet, you really shouldn't be eating it—because you're eating an animal that lived on shit. Literally. An animal that was fed candy bars. It's not a joke. Even cows are fed shit, sawdust, and candy bars (the remnants from the floor of the candy factories). Pigs can eat anything. But you should know where your food's coming from—you should know what you're eating, because it isn't a myth that it makes a difference. It does make a difference what the thing that you're eating ate. So you need to think about the fact that as your countertop is being coated in salmonella, you're also eating poop.

—ALEXIS

Celebrate the Holidays Responsibly

Among my mother's many famous and infamous concoctions, the Christmas dinners of my childhood featured a majestically displayed rack of lamb (complete with chop frills) as the main course. When I was a child I loved this meal, served in our rarely used dining room with a fire in the fireplace, candles, and antique china that I proudly set on the table. As I got older, the meals seemed to become increasingly grand, and my feelings of excitement turned stale: elaborate preparations, overeating, and excess just weren't fun anymore.

Two important reports on the ecological impact of our contemporary food choices got me thinking again recently about those chop frills and overfull stomachs. And they made me reaffirm a decision I made twentysomething years ago to leave the lamb—and meat altogether—off my holiday table.

The first report by Food and Water Watch details how industrial animal agriculture has continued to tighten its stranglehold on America, replacing more sustainable and humane farms with massive factory farms that endanger public health. The average size of U.S. hog factory farms, for example, increased by 42 percent between 1997 and 2007, and the number of cows on factory farm dairies nearly doubled in the same period. Farm Forward, an organization that opposes factory farming and works with traditional farmers to create alternatives to it, has determined that 99 percent of all animals raised in the United States now live their lives on factory farms.

The result? According to a second report by Environment America, "pollution from agribusiness is responsible for some of America's most intractable water quality problems—including the 'dead zones' in the Chesapeake Bay, Gulf of Mexico and Lake Erie, and the pollution of countless streams and lakes." Factory farms are also major contributors to the increasing risk of food-borne illness in the United States—poultry has been and remains the number one culprit. Factory farms fuel the growth of antibiotic-resistant bacteria, and they cause unthinkable suffering for animals.

Most of us eat to excess, especially during the holidays. Today I'm all about simplicity—less food, less stress, less waste—all year round. When I removed meat from my holiday table back in the 1980s, I also removed it from my daily diet.

No single dietary change I've made has had a more positive impact on my health. Last Christmas I prepared homemade pasta with truffles, risotto with mushrooms, and lots and lots of salads. It's never too late to make sensible changes to our holiday traditions, and when we change the holiday table, it can have a surprising ripple effect. My new holiday traditions are healthier, less wasteful, and less expensive. They contribute to my well-being and are better for the planet. Isn't that what the holidays are all about?

—ALEXIS

3

Getting Married in a Gray Flannel Suit

Alexis and Jennifer on Marriage and Relationships

The [Koppelman-Hutt] wedding at the family's Stanford White estate in Roslyn Harbor on Long Island was planned by the bride's mother, Bunny Koppelman, who is well known for her grand gestures. No one wanted to miss it: 500 guests were invited, and only 11 declined. The ceremony took place in a replica of Central Synagogue, on East 55th Street. The wooden imitation was designed by Robert Isabell and built over the family swimming pool. As trumpets played, pink doors swung open and the bride appeared in a John Anthony gown and overcoat with a long beaded train that sounded like crashing waves as she walked down the aisle. . . . David Fritz, the bride's brother-in-law, described the tent's decor as "a cross between a Persian den of decadence and a Beverly Hills Hotel cocktail party."

New York Times, *June 15, 1997*

∽

My friends are impatient to see how my twenty-one-year-old daughter Alexis will be married, but I already know it will be an event beyond my present imagination because her individualism and style will be expressed in some surprising new way. Nonetheless, I fantasize about a background of roses and a benediction of apple blossoms, and continue to perfect a possible setting for her. In the last two years, on the grounds at the back of the house, I've designed and built a network of trellises, inspired by the ironwork at Monet's *Giverny*. Soon they will be covered with garlands of old roses, completely enclosing the garden and creating an ideal private and perfumed world for 150 wedding guests.

Martha Stewart, Weddings (*1987*)

I spent an afternoon with Alexis shopping for her wedding suit. She decided to wear gray flannel. And there were to be virtually no guests. I worried that I would not be invited. But I was and was allowed to plan a wedding luncheon and order flowers and cake.

Martha Stewart, Martha Stewart Living, *December 1997*

When I got divorced I decided I would never squabble with anyone again. And then I thought, God, you'd lose your whole personality if you don't squabble.

Martha Stewart, April 9, 2010

Y ou don't have to get married if you don't want to.

Men who don't get married are hot and can have any girl they want, but if women don't get married there's something wrong with them. We're not antimarriage. We just don't think that getting married is the best thing in the world and not getting married is the worst thing in the world. Whether you're single or married, you're going to be happy some of the time and miserable some of the time. As the Buddha said, "Life is suffering." As far as we know, marital status has nothing to do with it.

A lot depends on your expectations of marriage. While Jennifer knew that marriage meant full commingled, cohabiting, co-everything coupledom—sharing the bedroom, sharing the bathroom, sharing everything—Alexis was a little thrown off by the fact that she had to actually *live* with the guy. Alexis thinks Jennifer's a freak because she likes being married and because she and her husband were basically attached at the hip for a long time, and Jennifer thinks Alexis is a freak because Alexis's idea of a perfect mate is someone with such a dangerous job he could die at any moment.

Marriage definitely isn't for everybody, and it better be for both people in the marriage or it won't last. Anybody who says that living with another person is easy and a walk in the park twenty-four hours a day, seven days a week, is lying or not present in their marriage. You're either someone who's interested in living a married life or you're not. Jennifer is that person, and right now, Alexis isn't.

Emotional barnacle, misanthropic hermit—whatever. There's plenty of shame no matter who you are and what you're looking for. So when it comes to getting married, living together, or staying single, figure out what you want, accept yourself, and live your life.

Just Because You Don't Want to Get Married Doesn't Mean You're a Freak Show

I was married once, for seven years. But we actually lived together for only six months. We knew each other for a very short period before we got married. He was my attorney—the one I hired to torture a guy who was torturing me—and because he's ultraethical he didn't want to date me until I was no longer his client. Eventually, after we got involved, he gave me a nickname, Lady Tourette, because I couldn't keep my mouth shut and I constantly commented on people's attire and behavior.

We couldn't live together at first because we lived in separate towns. I had a job in the Hamptons, so I couldn't *just leave*—and one day he basically said, "Okay, so you're moving to New York next week, right?" And we had a huge fight—complete with arguing at a restaurant table and people elbowing each other so everyone could look—which was *lovely*. I guess we should've had the Talk before that. All I can say is you should definitely live together before you get married.

My mother likes him. She even went to his wedding when he got married again after me. He's a really good guy. He's great, actually. He was too good for me. It just didn't work out. I was a bad wife.

Before I got married, I never thought about getting married. I didn't care one way or the other. It wasn't something I wanted or didn't want.

I just don't understand the institution of marriage. So you give someone a ring. That's nice. Does it have to be blessed by the state? If that's what you want, great. But I don't think you need to have it. It doesn't mean I wouldn't like to be so in love with someone that I'd want to marry him—I certainly would, I'd love that. But that hasn't happened, and I can't really say it bothers me that much.

—ALEXIS

Just Because You and Your Husband Are Inseparable Doesn't Mean You're a Freak Show

My husband and I are definitely into spending time together. When we first met, from the minute my husband and I started seeing each other seriously, he never left my apartment. We were constantly together. He even had his own apartment that he didn't give up until we were engaged. In the first two years of our relationship, we didn't have a single night apart. Spending too much time apart would give me tremendous anxiety. I'm extremely needy. But my husband needs me, too. So it works.

—JENNIFER

Jennifer and her husband, Keith, at her twenty-sixth birthday dinner
at the 21 Club in New York City.

You Can Never Have Enough Space in a Relationship

The only thing I'm needy about in a relationship is space. Spending time apart from someone I'm seeing is imperative for me. I can't be with someone who has to be with me all the time. I don't know if it's nature or nurture—but I *was* an only child. I never shared a room (except maybe for a couple of semesters in boarding school), and I'm comfortable being by myself. There are plenty of people who can't be by themselves, but I'm not one of them. I don't get bored; I don't get particularly lonely, for better or for worse, and I can always find something to do with my time.

I like to read. If I can't have that time when no one's there, then I start to lose it. I'm not sure there'll ever be a person that

I'd ever feel *so* comfortable with that I won't need time to myself. Plenty of relationships I've had might have lasted longer, but every time I turned around when I was dating someone it seemed like they were always standing right there. And I'd want to scream! "Go find something to do!" They'd ask me what we were going to do that weekend and I'd say, "I don't know. *I'm* reading. What are *you* doing?" I don't want everything to be "together." I want someone who likes to do his own thing.

Not seeing someone every day doesn't have to mean rejection. It's just that I need someone who also needs time apart. You need what you need. It's okay. It shouldn't mean you're a freak, even though people think you are if you like to be alone. To me, it's weird when people want to go to the gym together and do everything together. Really? You're not afraid of getting annoyed and sick of each other? You're separate people! You have to be able to have your own life! He may not be there forever. There has to be some happy medium between "We love each other and we're a couple" and "I can't live without him."

—ALEXIS

My Mother Used to Ask Keith What His Intentions Were

When Keith and I got involved, we were together twenty-four hours a day. My mother was so happy that I was protected by a big strong man that it didn't bother her that we were living in sin and doing God knows what. When she called the apartment and he was there, she'd say, "So Keith! Are you going to marry her? What are your intentions!?" And my sister, who lived at home at the time, would get on another extension and tell Keith, "Ignore her! You don't have to answer her!" Keith rolled with it because he was in it for the (very) long haul.

—JENNIFER

Alexis and Jennifer on the Ring

Jennifer likes jewelry that has meaning. She also cares about what jewelry looks like. So she's not going to wear something she doesn't like just because it has meaning. That's why Jennifer changed the setting of her engagement ring two times. Alexis makes fun of her because of the multiple resettings, but Jennifer wants to be clear on one very important point: she kept the diamond—she just changed the aesthetic.

This is what happened: Jennifer's fiancé, Keith, picked out the first setting. It was very plain—a gold band with platinum around the diamond. But Jennifer didn't like the two-tone nature of it. It was ever so slightly cheesy. The second time, Jennifer's mom took her ring and had it reset right before she got married. Jennifer changed that second setting because it was too fancy. So technically there were three settings: the one Keith picked out, the one Jennifer's mother picked out, and then the one Jennifer herself picked out.

Alexis doesn't care about the meaning when it comes to jewelry. All that matters to her is that it looks good. Maybe a man should give the woman he's proposing to a diamond wrapped up in a little note: "Let's go and set it!" That's an idea, right, boys? That way someone like Jennifer could pick out exactly what she wants the first time around. The only problem with giving a girl a loose diamond is that she can't put it on her finger right away—which means she can't walk around the restaurant and show it off to everybody.

Or walk around her apartment and tell her mother all about it over the phone, the way Jennifer did.

I Got Married in a Gray Flannel Suit Instead of a Wedding Dress

I like pretty dresses, so occasionally I would look at wedding dresses in magazines and store windows. But I didn't look at them in the "I can't wait to get married so I can wear that" sense. And then when I did in fact get married, I wore a gray flannel suit, so go figure. Why did I wear a gray flannel suit? Honestly? I was living in the Hamptons, and I had managed to

Alexis on her wedding day, with Martha.

allot myself one day—literally, eight hours, and I'm not exaggerating—to find myself something to wear in New York, get my hair colored, get a manicure and pedicure, and get a facial, and I couldn't find anything. I should have gone to Chanel and gotten a little Chanel suit, but I didn't. I ended up at Ralph Lauren. The suit was very fancy, but it was ugly. Maybe it wasn't ugly. It was just stupid. My husband was wearing a suit, so it was like two guys getting married, basically.

I had three guests. Not including the bride and the groom. We just had lunch. Five people all together. All my mother did the whole time, because she had one of the first digital cameras, was show the waiter her digital camera—every waiter who came by got a free digital camera jerk-off. That was the topic of conversation. Her new digital camera.

—ALEXIS

Why Have a Minimalist Wedding When You Can Have a Really Over-the-Top One?

It's so ironic that the daughter of the woman who wrote the book on weddings—literally—would have such a nonwedding wedding. Especially compared to my wedding—with my beaded ball gown, tons of people, a "mock synagogue" in our backyard, and the *New York Times* covering it. But, whatever.

—JENNIFER

It's Okay If You Loved Your Honeymoon (Even If You Don't Really Understand the Point of a Honeymoon)

I loved my honeymoon. We went to Italy and France for three weeks, but by the last four days I was ready to come home. When you're on a honeymoon you notice all of the other honeymooning couples, and you feel like you're being forced to go out and have a good time—which is weird because most of the time you've already lived together. If you've lived with someone for two years you're already *in* the relationship, in the thick of it, in the depths of it—you're like two years into the marriage already. The honeymoon used to be for people who didn't live together first and who weren't having sex—but now, you've been there, done all that already, so what's the point, other than to have a really fun vacation?

—JENNIFER

It's Okay If Your Honeymoon Was the Beginning of the End

The idea of a honeymoon was very oppressive to me. You're having a honeymoon with someone you already know and couldn't know any better already? I mean, *come on.* You might love each other, but you didn't just meet. The "honeymoon period" of your relationship is probably long over by the time you're on your actual honeymoon—which is my point: there is no point of a honeymoon. For my honeymoon I just wanted to stay in the Hamptons, but we ended up going to—where the hell did we go?

We were in the Hamptons for a while and then we went to Maine. My mother had just purchased her house in Maine, so we went there, and it wasn't very comfortable—she'd bought it completely furnished, so it was completely furnished with someone else's ugly furniture. Just getting the TV to work so we could watch a movie was hard—and when you're in Maine, you actually need to watch movies because there's not a lot to do. Basically, it was a couple of weeks of stress. It was probably the beginning of the end for both of us.

—ALEXIS

B ig wedding, small wedding.
Giant beaded wedding dress, stupid gray flannel suit.

Honeymoon, no honeymoon.

Marriages work out or they don't.

Jennifer's did. Alexis's didn't. Despite that, and despite the fact that the two of us are wired completely differently when it comes to how much space we need in a relationship—Alexis needs tons; Jennifer needs (almost) none—we still want the same things from a committed relationship:

Loyalty, new-and-improved rules for those who cheat, and a Celebrity Shtup List.

Stand by Me

The person you need to find in your life is someone who stands up for you and who stands by you. You go to a party and you're an asshole, and he'll stand by you. He'll tell you later that you were an asshole, but he won't tell you there at the party in front of other people. He'll stand up for you there and then later on he can say, "Honey? I can't be with you if you're gonna be an asshole." Otherwise, what are you doing with him?

So if your boyfriend or your husband looks at you like you're crazy when you say something at a party, you need to have a talk: "I'm sorry I was an asshole, but if you love me, you stand up for me—you love me *and* all my screwups, which you knew about before you married me, so it's not like it's a new thing. Should I work on them? Sure. I promise I will."

It's a two-way street. But you can't tell your significant other in front of other people that he's an asshole. You can't shame him. Unless you want a divorce. Then you can shame him all you want.

—ALEXIS

The Irresistibility-to-Annoyingness Ratio

I'm not easy to live with. I'm funny and warm and devoted, but I can be obnoxious and condescending. Keith says I have a part of me that's superirresistible and another part that's super-annoying, and the key is keeping the right ratio. Another key is for me to be less neurotic. Our biggest arguments have always been about health and safety. If I can't get my husband on the phone or if he doesn't answer the intercom in the house quickly enough, I think he's dead or severely injured. Craziness. We fight about the kids because I'm such a neurotic. If I think he's not being protective enough, he always says, "Do you really think I love them any less?"

Recently when we went on vacation to Hawaii, Keith and the kids went really far out in the water to swim with wild dolphins. I went crazy on the beach. "Today's the day!" I told my father. "Today's the day we're getting divorced!" When they got back to the beach, I went ballistic on my husband, who smiled at me and said being out in the ocean was incredible. And then

Alexis's Ridiculous Interview with Larry King

Larry King: Tonight, exclusive, Martha Stewart's daughter, Alexis Stewart, her first television interview ever. Great pleasure to welcome you. What are Alexis's goals? You're a young, beautiful woman. Do you want to have health spa salons around the country?

Alexis Stewart: I'm not so goal oriented.

I looked at my son: he was *so happy*. Swimming with dolphins and hearing them sing underwater was the highlight of his trip. And I loved my husband again.

—JENNIFER

A Husband Who Says He's Not Attracted to Other Women Is a Liar

The husband who will never admit to his wife that he finds another woman attractive or hot is a real problem. Because it just isn't true unless he's gay. He's *supposed* to think women are hot! He's *supposed* to have some sort of fantasy life. I don't need to know the details of it. I don't want to know the details of it! The less information, the better. But I know that my husband thinks Jennifer Aniston is hot, and I know he likes her better than he likes Angelina Jolie.

—JENNIFER

My Mother Advised Me Not to Have a Rich Ugly Guy's Baby

A woman who lived near us when I was little had married someone very wealthy and very unattractive, and my mother actually told me when I was a small child, "Now Alexis, if this ever happens, you make sure you have sex with somebody else to have *their* baby. Don't have *his* baby." She was very practical about it. It was a survival skill: you have someone rich and ugly who takes care of you, and you have someone who's hot and makes attractive babies.

But now you can't even marry the rich guy to take care of you and have the hot guy's baby because of DNA testing!

—ALEXIS

Here's the thing: trying to be friends with somebody's spouse—or with an ex—is a farce. It just is.

Alexis wasn't sure she agreed that you can *never* be friends with someone of the opposite sex, because her girlfriend got married when they were both around twenty-five, and Alexis would hang out with her friend's husband—without her friend. But after giving it some thought, Alexis remembered that she *did* sleep with her friend's husband, at some point, later on, so there goes that argument.

Jennifer has no doubt that being friends with other men when you're married simply isn't possible. In her opinion, the only way you can be friends with another man when you're married is if you find him so unattractive that there would be no way he could ever worm his way into your pants.

There's just no real male-female heterosexual friendship that doesn't have an underlying attraction. It doesn't mean you can't be friendly or "friends" with a coworker, but the minute the relationship extends beyond work, something else is holding it together. And we don't buy that it's going to stay strictly platonic, because even with the best of intentions things can go awry; even if you love your spouse or love the person to whom you're committed, putting yourself in that position is just foolish. Being married doesn't mean you don't want anybody else. Human beings have to make a choice to be monogamous. And that choice can be threatened if you're constantly in the face of somebody you want.

Is Jennifer friendly with her friends' husbands? Sure. Does Jennifer have an occasional text message with one of her friends' husbands that has to do with one of her friends or dinner plans as couples? Sure. Does she immediately copy and paste and send the message to her friend so she's aware of it? All the time.

How Jennifer and Keith Watch TV

Keith and I watched *30 Rock* recently on our DVR. The show is twenty-two minutes, we fast-forwarded through the commercials, yet somehow it takes forty-five minutes to watch a half-hour sitcom. Why? Here's the breakdown:

Watch a few minutes, then . . . pause to pee.

Watch a few minutes, then . . . pause for a discussion about characters.

Watch a few minutes, then . . . pause for rewinding and rewatching a funny part.

Watch a few minutes, then . . . pause for bickering.

Watch a few minutes, then . . . pause to kick the kids out of our room.

Watch a few minutes, then . . . pause to grope.

Pause to get a snack.

Finally finish the damn show.

Jennifer's just not interested in that kind of messing around. That's not how she's sinking her ship.

Alexis, on the other hand . . .

You're Not the Only One Who Cheated on Someone Who Was Already Being Cheated on and Got "the Lecture"

I was seeing a guy for a week or two—I'll call him David. He introduced me to his really fun friend, Chris, and his fun friend's wife and kids. Eventually I started seeing Chris when his wife wasn't around and when David wasn't around. And we really liked each other. A lot. He felt guilty, and then he had "problems," and then his wife found out about it and she came and gave me the Lecture. You know: "Chris is very charming, and he's this, and he's that, but he's got problems and you shouldn't be doing this." I just let her talk. And maybe that annoyed her—that I didn't scream back—but I didn't.

Then it turned out that she'd been shtupping David long before Chris and I got together. So don't come lecture me when you've been cheating on your husband and shtupping the guy I was seeing—and shtupping every guy you could get your hands on long before I'd met and started shtupping your husband!

—ALEXIS

Being Friends with an Ex Is a Farce

It's all well and good to be Facebook friends with an ex—but do *not* start interacting. Because all that's going to lead to is a long walk down memory lane. And you know the book *If You Give a Mouse a Cookie*? Well, if you take a walk down memory lane, you're gonna talk about sex. And if you talk about sex, you're gonna wanna have sex. So what's the point? Everyone changes the dynamic of the story of how a relationship ended, unless there was some sort of horrible betrayal—and even in those situations, I'm not convinced you can't get roped back in to old behaviors. It's just a bad idea, and everyone is susceptible to it. That doesn't mean there's something wrong with you. It just means you're normal.

When I was a newlywed I couldn't understand how you could even look at another man and think, OMG he's hot. I couldn't wrap my head around it. Back then, my husband was twenty-eight and I was twenty-five. But now I'm forty-one. So first of all, I'm sexually liberated and now I can only have sex with my husband, so what kind of sick joke is that? And he's hot—my husband is *hot*—and he's great. I *love* him. I live for him. But it doesn't mean that I'm not attracted to other men. We're wired to look around and fuck around. And we are wired to be able to choose to resist those urges, so why play with fire? You can't be in someone's life day to day and not expect old feelings to reemerge.

—JENNIFER

Confession Booth: I Hog the Covers

Apparently I roll over, wrap the comforter around me, and leave my unlucky guest uncovered and freezing to death. Shocking, right?

—ALEXIS

- *If you're going to cheat, don't get caught.* You'll be exposed as a liar and a cheat and you'll actually hurt the person you're cheating on.

**Alexis and
Jennifer's Rules
for Cheating**

- *If you cheated, shut up.* If you cheat and tell, you're an asshole. And the person you told should break up with you. Immediately. Because if you cheat and tell, then not only are you selfish and mean, you're also cruel. And if you're selfish and mean and cruel, you're probably not going to make a good boyfriend or girlfriend. The telling doesn't make sense to us. Telling is the most bizarre behavior that men have. And the excuse that "I needed to get it off my chest" is the most self-serving excuse there is. Tell me you don't like me anymore! Why would you possibly have to tell me that you're sleeping with someone else? It's only punishment. You feel the need to punish me? The excitement of cheating should be plenty. You got your rocks off, so shut up. Really. *Shut. Up.* Telling is nasty, cruel, bizarre, rude, unfathomable, and, quite frankly, weird. We don't get it.

- *Take your cues from women: women may cheat, but they don't tell.* They don't take the extra step of being mean. Women who fuck around will fuck around, but they'll be quiet about it.

- *If you cheated, don't tell unless you're asked.* As someone who's cheated, Alexis believes you should tell the truth about your cheating only if you know your primary relationship is over and the person you cheated on has *actual* proof of the cheating, so a denial is pointless. If you cheat, all bets are off. Unless you can come to some kind of agreement after that, you've ruined the relationship. It'll never be the same. When I was caught cheating once and the guy confronted me, I said, "Well, you better pack your bags and go." He couldn't believe that I wasn't going to beg him to stay. But why would I? It wasn't going to work out! I could have pretended and stayed with him for a while, but the relationship was never going to go anywhere. It was never going to go where he wanted it to go, because I didn't like him enough. I tried not to be cruel, but he wanted me to say that I was never going to do it again, and I couldn't say it. It would have been a lie and prolonged his suffering.

- *Every couple needs a Celebrity Shtup List.* A Celebrity Shtup List is a list of celebrity hotties you're allowed to have sex with, even though you're married. It's like a free pass. A get-out-of-jail-free card. Five famous people who don't count. Better hope your significant other doesn't become famous!

4

Not a Hoarder, Still a Slob

Alexis and Jennifer on Cleaning and Organizing

Life is too complicated not to be orderly.

Martha Stewart

⤜⤴

I'm a minimalist. I grew up with so much stuff that I went the other way. There were dishes piled eight feet high in every closet. My mother would go to tag sales constantly. She owns hundreds of tablecloths. It was too much. I couldn't take it anymore. I had to have nothing. Some might find my decorating style "austere" and I'd agree. It's cold. But at least there's no clutter.

Alexis Stewart

⤜⤴

You need to be ready to take care of any issue that arises in your bathroom at any moment—pee, poop, whatever. You see it, you clean it. There's no waiting. And I don't believe the people who say they don't see it.

Jennifer Koppelman Hutt

～✑

Alexis loves to clean way more than me. She lives in a 4,000-square-foot apartment and she doesn't have a housekeeper. She has the harnesses and can get out on the outside of the sloping roof and clean the windows.

Martha Stewart, Wall Street Journal, *December 3, 2009*

W ho was it who said your home is a reflection of your psyche? Martha Stewart? Probably.

If it's true, then Alexis's psyche is one serene, smooth, sparse place. And Jennifer's is all comfy and cozy.

Whether you live in a studio apartment or a mansion, and no matter how you choose to decorate it, your day begins and ends at home. Don't you want it to be a place that reflects you as a person? If a cluttered house reflects unsavory truths about its owner's emotional well-being—or lack thereof—then by not cleaning up, you're putting your own craziness on display. Do you really want people to know—immediately upon stepping through your front door—what a lunatic you are? Wouldn't it be better to keep your psychological imbalance contained for as long as possible?

Some people wonder if there's a gene for clutter. Hoarding is a form of obsessive-compulsive disorder (OCD), and, like other forms of OCD, it runs in families. But most of the time, what ails people when it comes to keeping their homes or cars clean isn't a hoarding gene. It's laziness. And time management problems. And denial. How else do you explain how people who are clean live with filthy kitchens and bathrooms and cluttered closets and cabinets?

Shame is a powerful motivator, so wanting to look normal might be an incentive for keeping your house from becoming a complete disaster. But a better incentive would be to keep your house clean and organized because that's the best way to live. In other words: do it for yourself.

While we differ on the belief that *cleaning* and *organizing* are relative terms—Alexis is obsessive and compulsive when it comes to cleaning, and she *loves* to clean; Jennifer isn't and doesn't—on this we completely agree: there's no excuse for failing at minimal housekeeping.

True Confession: I Dated a Hoarder

I dated a hoarder before I knew what one really was (that is, before there was a TV show by that name). I'd go to his place and think, What is wrong with you? It's ugly! It's dirty! It's spoiled! It's broken! And you still refuse to get rid of it? He went to China for a few weeks, and while he was gone I cleaned his house—especially his kitchen. It took twelve hours to clean a room that was only six feet by six feet, and I wasn't even completely done. He had $970 in change that he wouldn't take to the bank. You mean to tell me that exploding shoe box full of change is making you happy? I dated him for about nine months, but it felt like a year because he never left my apartment—I guess living in the middle of a hoard isn't that fun after all.

He didn't do anything. It was bizarre. He was like a girl. I'd get home and he'd say, "So what are we doing for dinner?" And I'd say, "Did you do anything today? Did you leave the house? Did you clean your apartment?" He'd always say the same thing: "Time got away from me."

I'm fascinated by hoarders, especially the most famous hoarders on the planet: the Collyer brothers, Lusk and Langley. They were wealthy brothers who lived up in Harlem in the early 1900s at the corner of Fifth Avenue and 128th Street, and they went nuts. They hoarded, and they were also afraid of people breaking in, so their house was full of booby traps. They collected a hundred tons of rubbish, and eventually one of the brothers became bedridden, so the other brother took care of him. But the caretaker brother tripped his own booby trap, and all of these newspapers and things fell on him and he died. The other brother then starved to death. It took days for anyone to get into the house because the brothers had so much stuff, including around twelve to fifteen grand pianos.

Martha's a little bit of a hoarder. She won't let go of anything. She won't even sell things that she's never going to use. She takes things from New York City, then puts them in her house in Westchester. Then she takes them back from Westchester to the city again, then she puts them in the Hamptons, and then she hires another truck that takes it to Maine. Then she changes her mind, and it keeps going. It never stops, and it goes around and around—in some weird way she thinks she's saving money because she's not wasting anything.

—ALEXIS

Alexis Loves to Clean (Even without Drugs)

I do all my own cleaning. I find it very therapeutic, and it's good exercise. Or so I keep telling myself. I'll do almost anything to get something clean: I've even rappelled down my skylights to clean them. I hate Swiffers for dusting because they're wasteful and flimsy, and I love Rubbermaid microfiber products because they're washable and sturdy. To clean the floors, I use some neutral unscented cleaner.

Rags and a bucket are the only way to go. I actually buy rags by the dozen from a hotel supply company. I can't believe that people who don't like to clean *never* get in the mood to clean. To me that's weird. You'd think that sometimes you'd get that urge. So if you don't, then drugs are the answer.

—ALEXIS

W hen you're Martha Stewart's daughter—the vault of all homekeeping knowledge—cleaning isn't a big deal. For the rest of us, of course, it's a huge deal. Where do we start? How do we do it? Can we lie down and have a cookie yet? For Alexis, keeping her house clean isn't rocket science—and it's even good exercise.

Of course, let's be frank: most people are never going to be as crazy as that—to love cleaning and think of it as part of a fitness regimen—but we can heed Alexis's advice, which starts with this: "Don't go crazy with the germ-killing—Americans are too goddamn clean anyway."

That said, both Alexis and Jennifer don't believe there's any excuse for visible dirt. Or any excuse not to wash your hands. Or to leave pee on the toilet seat. Alexis has boiled down the rest of how to keep your bathroom from getting completely disgusting and how to keep cleaning from becoming or remaining an overwhelming and impossible chore into three steps.

Alexis's Three Easy Steps to a Clean Bathroom

1. *Don't wear gloves.* Sorry, but you can't get anything clean with a big pair of rubber gloves on.

2. *Decant environmentally friendly products into plain spray bottles, then label them with P-Touch labels.* Label one spray bottle "General Cleaner"; label another "Glass." Let them sit on the edge of your bathtub so whenever you need them, they're right there. All you need to do is spritz the toilet, the bathtub, or the sink and wipe it with a rag.

3. *Be green while you clean: use rags.* Have a little basket or bin under the sink that's just for rags, and every time you use one, toss it in the bin. Then wash them. You can also just use paper towels (unbleached, of course), but using rags lets you clean and be green at the same time.

There's always the part in every section where our true craziness is revealed—where we share, voluntarily, and without shame, our idiosyncrasies, neuroses, and bizarre pathologies. For this topic—cleaning and organizing—the two of us may differ on degrees of neatness, but we're certifiable when it comes to our shared need for extreme cleanliness verging on germophobia, mothers who hated trash and trash cans, our supersensitivity to (artificial) scents, and our deep disdain for potpourri. Whether it's the way we were born or how we were raised—nature or nurture, whatever—it's one of the few topics we have in common, and that alone is worth celebrating.

Alexis's library.

Joan Crawford Redux: No Trash in the Trash Cans Ever!

I'm sure this will surprise you, but my mother's a little crazy about trash in the kitchen: there can never be *any* trash in the garbage can. We went from No Trash Can in Any Room Other Than the Kitchen to You Don't Ever Put Anything in the Trash Can. Most of my life it was No Trash Can. But now my mother has graduated to Take Out All the Trash to the Bin Outside Every Half Hour. And, frankly, now I can only tolerate trash in the kitchen bins.

What do they say about apples and trees?

—ALEXIS

Even Though There Are Trash Cans in Every Room

My mother had the same issue with trash cans. There were trash cans in every room in my family's house—*every* room, *every* bathroom, everywhere I looked. But we weren't allowed to use them.

—JENNIFER

Just Throw Away a Caterer's Leftovers

I get crazy about food preparation and hands touching food. I was at a party, and the food was great. Everyone was saying how delicious the food was and how great the caterer was. I was going to take home some string beans because there were tons of leftovers, so I'm in the kitchen with the hostess and she says to the chef, "My friend is going to take home some string beans." He says, "Great!" And then he proceeds to take his ungloved hand and shove it into the dish and grab a handful of string beans and put them in a ziplock bag. Then he grabs a second handful and puts them in the ziplock bag, and he hands me the bag. My friend starts giggling because she knows how neurotic I am, and of course I don't want to be rude to the chef to his face, but please. I'm not going to eat them, knowing his hands have been everywhere. So I left them there.

—JENNIFER

Unscented Is My Favorite Scent

My favorite scent is unscented. Your house shouldn't smell like anything, good or bad. It can smell like the delicious thing you're cooking, while you're cooking it or right after you cooked it, and it can smell like the cleaning products you just used, although I would prefer unscented. But other than that, it shouldn't smell like anything. It certainly shouldn't smell like some toxic artificially scented crap. I can't stay in someone's house if they have one of those candles—those cinnamon clove

The vanity in Alexis's bedroom.

apple turnover candles. They're vile and seriously strain my breathing talents.

—ALEXIS

People Who Use Those Christmas Tree-Shaped Air Fresheners in Their Cars Are Morons

And what about those Christmas tree–shaped air fresheners that taxi drivers hang from their mirrors? Now regular people hang them in their cars. They're disgusting. And toxic. What kind of parents hang them in the car when they're driving kids around all day? Morons. I don't like scented candles, either, but sometimes I'll boil some cinnamon, and that makes my house smell delightful. And it isn't toxic.

—JENNIFER

I Hate Potpourri

I hate potpourri. Either it smells too much or it doesn't smell at all and is dusty. I really hate Christmas potpourri. It's horrible. The potpourri my mother made had a million ingredients in it and used to be everywhere. It made me sick. The smell of cloves especially reminds me of my mother sitting me down with a giant bowl of oranges during the holidays and making me poke cloves into the oranges until my thumbs bled because cloved oranges made good Christmas gifts.

—ALEXIS

I always find potpourri confusing. I want to eat it because I think it's food: it's like nuts and berries and granola. When someone

What's Actually in Those Stupid Christmas Tree-Shaped Car Air Freshener Things?

The chemicals emitted from these cardboard air fresheners have been analyzed as potentially dangerous to humans. The most common chemical, phthalates, has been known to cause reproductive problems, hormonal abnormalities, and birth defects. Other known ingredients that cause serious health issues are formaldehyde, acetone, and terpenes. These chemicals contain pollutants that when mixed with ozone, cigarette smoke, or dust can cause breathing complications, headaches, and damage to the central nervous system.

What's in Martha's Potpourri

Cinnamon sticks
Dried orange peel
Fresh cloves
Cornflowers (bachelor's buttons)
Juniper berries
Lavender
Oil of freesia and lily of the valley
Orris root powder (to hold the essential oils together)

gives you a bag of potpourri as a gift, you have to pretend you like it—which is painful. And to make your own potpourri the way Martha did, you'd have to spend over $500 in ingredients. I'd rather go into a potpourri store and buy it already made. Or take the $500 and spend it elsewhere—like on shoes!

—JENNIFER

You Can Put a Duvet Cover on a Comforter without Actually Getting inside It

There's no easy way to put a duvet cover on a comforter, but you don't actually have to get inside it. First, you open the bottom of the duvet cover. Then you fold the duvet and you have the two top corners in your other hand and you shove that inside. Put one corner of the duvet into one corner of the cover, grab it on the outside, then put the other corner in the other corner and grab it on the outside. Then you shake, shake, shake. It's not that hard (although reading over these instructions makes me dizzy and confused).

—ALEXIS

Alexis's lipstick collection (it's quite a collection for someone who almost never wears lipstick).

True Confession: I Iron My Sheets
(and So Does My Mother)

Sometimes I sleep on linen sheets. Linen is very wrinkly after washing. If you hang them up to dry, they're way too stiff and itchy (I tried that once and had to strip the bed at one o'clock in the morning and wash them again). I have a Miele rotary iron, so ironing sheets is much quicker than you think: it takes about an hour to iron two sets of sheets, a duvet cover, and four pillowcases.

Cotton sheets especially come out smooth and cool and look and feel cleaner for longer. I can't—*can't*—sleep on a "blend" or sheets that have been treated so they don't wrinkle. Of course, all of Martha's sheets are ironed, and she even has one of those contraptions at her house in Maine that irons an entire sheet flat in a single movement (it requires two people to operate).

—ALEXIS

Admit it, one of the reasons you bought this book and are reading it now is to find out one of the most guarded secrets of the universe: how Alexis Stewart organizes her house.

Not how Martha organizes her house—you can see that on TV any day—but the pared down, distilled, demystified, minimalist version of all of Martha's teachings. Sure, you wanted to hear Alexis's shtupping stories and find out what her childhood was like, but home organization is your true fetish. There's no shame in that. Especially with Alexis—whose level of neatness and organization could be considered fetishistic, too.

So you've come to the right place. This is what you've been waiting for (and what you paid for).

You want to get organized? Here's how you start:

1. Empty.

2. Sort.

3. Put the crap you never use or wear in clear plastic containers. Or better yet, give it away!

For everything else you use and want to keep, all you need is one magic item (or a few thousand of them): the Container Store shoe box, sweater box, and boot box! Sort of like Tupperware for your closet, these clear plastic boxes allow you to see what's inside, neatly organized, without having to open them up. Use them to organize almost everything in your house.

Alexis and Jennifer on Martha

Associated Press: What are some of your favorite Martha moments from TV?

Jennifer: There's one where she does a linen closet and tacks labels in tiny frames on each shelf. It's just so over the top. It was her dream to have this perfect linen closet. And there's an episode where Martha teaches somebody how to load a dishwasher.

Alexis: I like when she demonstrates how to transport a potted plant while wearing Hermes pants and uses enough packing material to move a whole house. But we're just moving one plant. Really, you just put the plant in a truck and drive.

AP: How do you think your mother got her reputation?

Alexis: I think it's something that started without her. It started, I think, as an envy thing, and she makes you feel inadequate, so it's easy to think that she doesn't have a sense of humor, and it has never been her intention to make anyone feel that way. It's only her intention to teach, which can be irritating. But if you're tuning in, that's what you're looking for.

- *Sweaters.* Store your sweaters in clear plastic boxes and they'll be protected from moths *and* look neat on your shelves. If you want extra credit, arrange your sweaters by color, according to the spectrum. No, this will not make you seem like a psycho. Maybe OCD, but not psychotic.

- *Underwear.* Separate your special-occasion undies from the everyday ones. We don't mean you should put all the fancy ones in there—by all means, wear the black demi to parent-teacher conferences, no one will know—just that you shouldn't let scary girdles and ridiculous strapless bras hog space in your underwear drawer.

- *Scarves.* Arrange a bunch of scarves by color so you can find the one you're looking for at a moment's notice.

- *Bills.* Put all of your bills in one folder, the ones due first in front. If you want to delay till the last minute, put a stamp on the envelopes, stick a return address label on them, and write the due date on the front so you know at a glance when to pay.

- *Photos.* File loose photos until you get around to putting them in a scrapbook or making one of those online photo albums. *If you ever get around to putting them in a scrapbook or making one of those online photo albums.*

"There's gotta be a shade of eye shadow that will change my life!"
—Alexis

- *Christmas cards.* Collect Christmas cards by year. Label boxes with a label maker—Brother makes a good one—and use a cute font. Then, after you've done all this work, go ahead and throw them away. You'll be sick of looking at them by then.

You Don't Have to Be Rich to Have Organized Closets

Most people we know who have disgusting closets claim they don't have enough cash to hire a custom closet company. "Of course your closets are neat, girls," they say, "you're gazillionaires!" First, we're not, and second, you don't need custom teak shelving or motorized racks to be organized. You don't even need to drop a few hundred at the Container Store if you can't afford to. All you need are a few basics:

- *Aluminum shelving.* Go to Costco or online to www.uline.com and buy a few sets of aluminum shelving. It's easy to assemble and dirt cheap. Then line all of the walls in your closet with the shelving and space the shelves at different heights to accommodate different items, from all of your clear boxes full of treasures to stacks of folded T-shirts.

- *Fold everything.* We think folded items are much easier to see on a shelf than stuffed in a drawer. Plus everything looks better when it's folded. If you're not sure how to properly fold things like sweaters, shirts, sheets, or towels, there's probably a YouTube video that'll show you what to do, or you can check Martha Stewart's website. Or you can just go to the Gap or J.Crew and watch the salespeople fold things all day.

- *Devote one whole shelf to your makeup.* You know, the makeup that should be organized in clear Lucite containers and cups atop a pretty tray. You don't want to keep your makeup in the bathroom where just any person can get to it. Plus, if you drop a bunch of lipsticks and compacts in there, even the most immaculate bathroom can look messy. Trust us, if there's any room that shouldn't look messy, it's the bathroom.

- *Decide on a shoe-storage plan.* Neither of us is a big fan of the *Sex in the City* shoebox-per-pair-of-shoes-that-you-keep-in-the-box, because it's such a waste of space, and not everyone has a place to put all of their shoes. But the problem is, shoes get dirty and dusty if they're on the floor, so either do the shoebox-with-a-photo thing, if you can deal with it—it keeps them clean and you can feel like Carrie Bradshaw, if that's something that appeals to you—or transfer your shoes into clear Container Store plastic boxes. Or get one of those things that hangs on the inside of your closet door for space-saving shoe storage.

- *Get matching hangers.* Whether they're the cheap Huggable Hangers that Jenny loves and that Alexis hates or the custom-made, special-order $10,000-per-order hangers Alexis has, make sure you have hangers that match. And plenty of them. Alexis doesn't even care if the hangers are plastic: just make sure your clothes don't fall off of them and that they're all uniform. It'll make you feel better.

For Those of You Taking Notes at Home: Clinical Terms for Filth-and-Home-Related Phobias

Fear of dust	amathophobia or koniophobia
Fear of disorder or untidiness	ataxophobia
Fear of microbes	bacillophobia
Fear of bacteria	bacteriophobia
Fear of slime	blemophobia
Fear of contamination	molysmophobia
Fear of germs	verminophobia
Fear of fecal matter	coprophobia or scatophobia
Fear of throwing anything away	disposophobia

1. *Make your bed every day.* We don't understand people who don't make their beds in the morning. What are you, ten years old? Twelve years old? Make your bed. Every day. Otherwise, why have linens? Why not just have a sleeping bag? Or a nest of twigs and branches? Or why not move back home? Don't live like an animal or worse, a child. Make your bed every day. In fact, if you're reading this and your bed isn't made, go make it right now.

2. *Clean your bathroom every day.* There's never an excuse to have a dirty bathroom. Ever. So clean it. Every day. It's unacceptable. And it has nothing to do with what your style is;

Alexis and Jennifer's No-Excuses Rules for Minimal Housekeeping

cleanliness is nonnegotiable. Bottom line: You need to be ready to take care of any issue that arises in your bathroom at any moment. If it's an issue of pee, poop, snot, blood—any bodily fluid—when you see any of it, you clean it. There's no waiting. Never! And we don't buy it when people say they don't see it. That's bullshit. Of course they see it. They just don't want to deal with it. If you're one of those people who doesn't want to deal with it, then hire someone to deal with it for you. A bathroom should be cleaned daily. Just wipe it down with some sort of germ-killing or soapy something. Teach your man how to clean up if no one taught him to before.

3. *Clean your kitchen.* It's the same thing as the bathroom: How can you leave a sink full of dirty dishes? Or a cutting board that has chicken juice all over it? We don't get it! And are people always having something with burned-on cheese that's soaking? Is *that* what everyone's eating *every* day, and is *that* why you're not washing your pan—because it's so crusted you can't possibly clean it? Most people have whatever they have—a sandwich, a vegetable, a salad—and do the dishes. It's easy. You eat! You wash the plate! Done.

4. *Don't leave dirty dishes and cereal bowls with the milk still in them in the sink.* What's keeping you from washing two dishes? Do you *really* want to have to wash fifty-eight crusty dishes later? Then there's something to dread when there shouldn't be anything to dread. It should take one minute. And what about the cereal bowl—people leave the cereal in the bowl in the sink, rotting. I mean, what is the deal? What's your problem? If you've had Cocoa Puffs, drink the milk. Why are you wasting that? Cap'n Crunch milk? They make ice cream out of that stuff now. In fact, you could gather up all your disgusting cereal milk and make ice cream out of it— the way Alexis collects all of the wine she doesn't drink to make her own red wine vinegar. In New York City (at Momofuku), people pay good money for cereal-flavored ice cream.

5. *Clean out your refrigerator and get rid of expired condiments (especially chutney, which shouldn't even be there in the first place).* We can't deal with people who don't clean out their refrigerators and have expired food in there and in their pantries: moldy bread and cereal from two years ago and pasta with bugs in the box. If you're over the age of twenty, you have to clean out your refrigerator. Every five or six months empty it out. Clear it out. Throw away what you haven't touched. We don't even understand how people let it get to that point in the first place—the point of being filled with unidentifiable food in various stages of rot and decay. But some people do, and we're not here to shame you. If you're one of those people, pick a time on your calendar—every September and March, say. Pick two days to do it, and if you can't do it yourself, if you're so anticleaning and you can't deal, then don't deal. Hire someone.

   As for condiments, these are the only ones you should have in your refrigerator or pantry: mustard, soy sauce, duck sauce, mayonnaise, and ketchup. (Alexis doesn't even think you need duck sauce, but Jennifer insists you need it for chicken fingers.) And they shouldn't be old and crusty and half-empty or anywhere close to their expiration dates. You shouldn't have any chutney—expired or otherwise. Nobody eats chutney. Chutney isn't even a real condiment!

6. *Steam-clean your microwave (assuming you own one, which, of course, Alexis doesn't).* What's with the dirty microwave? Are you living in Denny's? Or IHOP? You take a bowl with lemons and water and steam it for thirty seconds or a minute—the steam cleans the microwave walls so you can wipe down the inside with a damp cloth. Don't use cleaning spray inside the microwave, just a damp cloth.

7. *Lose the heated toilet seat.* It's completely incomprehensible to us why anyone would want a vinyl toilet seat. Or a heated toilet seat. We don't understand: you *want* the germs to grow?

Like, your ass is so delicate you can't even sit on a plastic toilet seat that never really even gets cold? You need it *heated* to a germ-loving temperature? What the hell is wrong with you? Get rid of it!

8. *Change your sheets at least once a week.* Listen, you have to change your sheets. Bare minimum: once a week. We prefer two times a week (max, though—don't go overboard unless there's a good reason, like you're ill). It doesn't have to be that complicated. Just don't have a bed with fifty layers and a hundred pillows. Keep it simple: use a bottom sheet, a top sheet, and a comforter that's washable or a duvet cover over a comforter. You can make it even simpler by having a duvet with a washable cover and a bottom sheet.

9. *Open your mail.* Or you're going to be sorry. Open it, recycle the waste, and put the rest in a pile. Every few days, file it. Alexis files everything. She has a file for every bill and every other category of paperwork, and then after she's procrastinated doing her taxes and files late, at least it's all there and it's in order.

    You get a bill from Con Ed, you pop it in the file, behind last month's Con Ed bill. Being organized is easy. Paying your bills and doing your taxes are completely different from being organized, because money triggers emotional issues for most people. Filing the receipt is easy, because you just set up your filing cabinet and then every year you pull all of that stuff out when you're done with your taxes, and you put it in a box with a label with the year on it. And there's the year you need in a box.

10. *Recycle.* We don't understand why people don't recycle. Look at it like a game. Figure it out. Try. It's not brain surgery. You can watch television and do it at the same time. That should be every American's dream. Or . . .

11. *If you don't care about living in filth, then embrace your filth.* Go ahead! Live with a dirty refrigerator! Be the freak who

actually makes yourself sick from a dirty refrigerator! If you don't care enough to clean your refrigerator, then be proud of your filth. If your house is that dirty, then there's something wrong with you. It could be that you perversely feel so privileged that you think you need not clean, but whatever the reason, if you don't want to change, accept yourself and ignore our scorn.

12. *Try to understand why filth doesn't bother you.* We believe that low self-esteem and a sense of giving up is at the root of all filth. Cleaning is part of taking care of yourself, and if you're feeling so low that you can't have a clean environment, then something is wrong. Or you're a hoarder. Either way, you're probably going to need more help than we can give you here in this mock self-help book, so you might want to contact a good therapist, a professional organizer, or even just a good cleaning person.

5

Should Sex Ever Involve Food?

Alexis and Jennifer on Sex and Dating

I like the things about sex the best.

Martha Stewart on texting lingo

∼

I never get to do anything in my dreams. I never get to open the presents or have sex with the guy. It's the story of my life.

Alexis Stewart

We're not going to beat around the bush—proverbial or otherwise. We agree on almost nothing when it comes to dating and casual sex.

Alexis thinks the best part of a date is getting ready for the date; Jennifer used to cry when she got ready for a date.

Alexis thinks there's something wrong if you don't sleep with someone on a first date; Jennifer thinks there's something wrong if you do.

We still don't understand why dating was harder for Jennifer than it was for Alexis; Jennifer's great with people and Alexis is horrible with people, so Alexis should have been the one to be scared and miserable on every date. Maybe it had less to do with Jennifer's "people skills"—or Alexis's lack thereof—and more to do with the fact that Jennifer worried about the date going well. Alexis never worried about whether a date was going well; she was probably too busy having sex already. And besides: Alexis didn't go on that many dates.

The trouble starts with the most fundamental dating question: Should you or should you not sleep with someone on a first date?

Jennifer never had sex on a first date.

Alexis always has sex on a first date if there is any chance of a second date. Alexis drinks; Jennifer thinks that makes the sex easier for her.

Jennifer thinks you should be attracted enough to the person to *want* to have sex on the first date but that you shouldn't *have* sex on the first date, and you should be able to wait—for four dates.

Alexis wants to know why there's a number involved when it comes to waiting for sex. Why isn't it a *feeling* you're waiting for? Why don't you wait until you feel like you want to have sex with someone—which means *first date*! And while Alexis could definitely have sober sex on a first date if she had to, why would she want to? She wants to have fun, and sober sex on a first date isn't fun!

With us, there's no one right way to be. If, like Alexis, your idea of fun is having sex with a virtual stranger on a first date, then fine, go ahead. Have sex with a virtual stranger on a first date! You're not the only one who likes that kind of thing. But if that's not your idea of fun, there's no shame in waiting, either. Alexis might think the point of a date is to have sex, but Jennifer thinks the point is to get to know someone. And there are lots of ways of get to know someone—talking, having dinner, going to a movie, showing your collection of Cabbage Patch dolls and Hello Kitty merchandise— that don't involve taking your clothes off and being naked.

Differences aside, our bottom lines are pretty much the same: Sleep with everyone you want to sleep with. Don't sleep with anyone you don't want to sleep with.

And have as much great sex before you're married as you can. Because once you're married, that's it! (At least, in Jennifer's opinion.)

You're Not the Only One Who Has Sex on the First Date (and Sometimes Marries the Guy)

To me, if you're not going to have sex on a first date, then I don't understand the point of the date. What better way is there to get to know someone than by having sex? If you don't have sex on the first date, it means you don't like the person enough to have sex. And having sex on the first date doesn't mean the relationship won't last. Every single guy I've ever dated I've slept with (or the equivalent) on the first date. Every. Single. One. Two-year relationships. Two-week relationships. I got married to the guy I slept with on the first date. When my ex-husband finally asked me out, he said we weren't going to have sex on our first date, and I said, "Oh, really?" Of course we had sex on our first date. And then we ended up getting divorced. But having sex on the first date had nothing to do with it.

How soon you have sex or how long you don't have sex for the first time is no guarantee that the relationship—or marriage—is ultimately going to work out. There's no guarantee when it comes to anything about relationships. It's either going to work out or it's not going to work out. And it's not just about sex—it's about having a good time, if possible, so if sex turns out to be part of it, *whatever*.

I don't think it matters when you sleep with someone. The pain that people experience is going to happen no matter what. You end up feeling the pain of rejection no matter when it happens, so you might as well try to have some fun.

—ALEXIS

It's Okay If Having Sex with a Virtual Stranger Isn't Your Thing

If having sex on the first date works for you, fine. It just didn't work for me because I couldn't separate sex from love. I thought if you wanted to have sex with me, how could you not love me? I couldn't wrap my head around the sex-is-just-sex thing. If sex isn't a big deal for you, then have sex as often and as much as you want. But if you're someone who can't disconnect sex from emotional attachment, then you have to be careful, and maybe it's better to wait. Not because he's not going to want to be in a relationship with you now that he's slept with you, but because it's not something you can handle. I think I would have felt worse if I'd slept with more of the guys that I liked. In the end, the point is knowing yourself—whether you're a sex-is-just-sex kind of person or a sex-is-love person.

Romantic
Jennifer and
Keith.

Because the other part of the point is minimizing your exposure to potential pain and misery.

I had dating rules only in college, and I had only one rule: I wasn't allowed to fool around with someone during the first week, because I'd get a reputation. So two weeks in, I'd be fooling around with someone. And by fooling around I mean making out. I was an "everything but" girl—I didn't think there was anything wrong with oral sex. Intercourse was what defined whether a girl was a slut or not. If there was no penetration, then it was all fair game. I didn't want to get a reputation, even though some women would kill for a reputation.

Where I was from, being called a slut was not a good thing. Alexis says that's such a Long Island thing. Ironically, every girl wants to be looked at like that—as a slut; you just don't want to be labeled one. Ultimately, all we want is to be found desirable. I didn't have sex with a lot of guys when I was dating because I didn't want to, and it took years before I had great sex and felt liberated and able to own my sexuality. You need that kind of experience before you get married, because if you've never experienced great sexual chemistry with someone, then how do you know?

—JENNIFER

Getting Ready for a Date

Here's the thing: the hours before the date are, by far, better than any date you will ever have. While you're getting ready for a date, you put your favorite music on, you drink your favorite drink, you put on your makeup and your best outfit for that occasion and your most flattering underwear, and you think about how fabulous you are. Just realize that the moment the doorbell rings and you answer it, it's going to be a steep downhill slide from there.

—ALEXIS

When I was single I hated dating. *Hated* it. It was too much pressure. I hated it so much that I'd cry before every date. Literally, tears. Getting dressed was a task that seemed insurmountable—to find the right thing to wear—like if he saw that my ass was big, it would be all over. Like he *wasn't* going to see it because I'd covered it up under a blazer? But that's what I thought: if I covered my ass with a blazer he wouldn't know it was big. Looking back, I think, OMG! What the hell was wrong with me? It's ridiculous, but so many women think exactly the same way. So for me, getting ready was the worst part.

Another one of my issues with dating was the game playing. I'd go out with a guy, and we'd sit at a table, and he'd tell me how much fun he was having, how much he liked me, and how he couldn't wait to go out with me the next time, even saying here's where we'd go and here's what we'd do—and then I'd never hear from him again. And I was flabbergasted! You said you liked me. Why did you say you liked me if you didn't, in fact, like me? I couldn't understand it or the whole I'm-just-going-to-pretend-I-like-you-and-never-call-you-again-even-though-I-said-I-was-going-to-call-you-again.

Dating always felt like an audition: one wrong move, and it's all over. I found the whole thing very stilted and sad and weird. I just didn't get the rules. You couldn't act like you liked someone until you knew for sure that he liked you, too. I couldn't do it right. I wasn't cool. I felt like the date was going to suck even before I left the house, even before I got my clothes on. So I would panic.

—JENNIFER

Jennifer and her husband make a good-looking couple, right?

Jennifer Thinks Alexis Should Try Online Dating

Jennifer: I can't believe you've never tried online dating. I find that so odd. You had a "dalliance" with a radio-show listener. You weren't afraid of being chopped up into teeny tiny little pieces by someone you'd never met?

Alexis: No. Not even remotely.

Jennifer: I was afraid for you. And that's my issue with online dating. The anonymity of it. Someone can pretend to be someone they're not. That's not your issue with it?

Alexis: No. I just can't do it. Someone would recognize me and be like "Martha Stewart's daughter is online dating!"

Jennifer: But in real life people would know you went on a date, so what difference does it make?

Alexis: Because I'm meeting the person before they know anything about me.

Jennifer: So you meet someone in a bar, and then they recognize you.

Alexis: I've never met anyone in a bar and then gone home with them. Okay, I did once. But he was gorgeous.

Jennifer: *Really?* You're the type who sees a guy at the supermarket and thinks to yourself, "He's hot. I'd like to have sex with him. Right now"?

Alexis: I saw someone at the supermarket right around the corner from here over three years ago and I'm still madly in love. I didn't only want to have sex with him that day. I wanted to marry him and have his babies.

Jennifer: So, let's say you met a hot guy online—

Alexis: No guy I would like is online dating. There's something wrong with him if he's online dating.

Jennifer: How do you know that? You don't know! I think you should give it a try.

Alexis: You'd like that, wouldn't you? That would be entertainment for you. You like the idea of me online dating in theory, but if I found someone online and told you I was going on a date with him, you'd be like "No! You can't! Because he might chop you up into little pieces!"

Jennifer: That's because you're not very discerning.

Alexis: I'm a big believer in pheromones. Huge.

Jennifer: Oh, okay. So you can't online date because you can't have Smell-O-Vision?

Alexis: Right! If there was Smell-O-Vision, I might be able to do it.

The world is full of bad-date stories and bad-sex stories. Between the two of us, we could fill up an entire chapter with our horror stories alone, but instead we've selected a few of our favorite dating stories to share along with a few confessions and a few important truths—to prove that you're not the only one who has (barely) survived the dating world.

One of Alexis's Great-Dates-That-Didn't-Work-Out Stories

One of the best dates I ever had was a daytime date. The guy worked on Wall Street, and we walked all the way home to his apartment on 75th and Park, and we stopped midway and went to the top of the Empire State Building. It was a summer weekday, it wasn't crowded, and it was beautiful weather—it was all fun—but I didn't really like him. It was a great date, but we didn't have sex. I mean, I can't always be the aggressor. It's so tiring.

He was strange, but then I like the strange ones. And he lived with his mother (we were young), and in the short time we dated we had one too many meals with his mother. In her apartment.

If you want me, make a move. Honestly, it's very strange when a guy doesn't make a move. It's like, dude, you can have it. It's free. We don't have to get married, so what are you waiting for? I think it's really indicative of something odd—either it's a power trip or he doesn't like you enough, or he's shy about sex—but then why spend time together?

—ALEXIS

One of Jennifer's Favorite Worst-Date Stories

I had a lot of bad dates, but my favorite was the time I went to a party and there was this guy there who I thought was really cute. After the party my friend said she'd find out if he liked me or if he had any interest in me, so the next day she called me and said he totally liked me and that she was going to fix us up.

So he calls me, and we talk, and I'm thinking that there's not that much there, but I keep remembering how cute he was, so I figure it will be fine. The night we have our date he shows up, and it's the wrong guy! So now, not only is it the wrong guy and I'm not at all attracted to him, but he also has no personality. There's nothing! I've just finished law school, and at dinner this moron is trying to convince me that the defense is "guilty by reason of insanity," and I say to him, "No, it's *not guilty* by reason of insanity." He's in the produce business, and he's telling me that *I'm* wrong. And I'm thinking, But I just finished law school! This is first-year law! This is remedial! You're a moron and you're ugly!

—JENNIFER

Sex That Involves Food

I was just reading a really good short story, and the guy and the woman had Nutella smeared on their chests. I don't understand sex with food. It's disgusting. And messy. And who's changing the sheets? Me, probably. And they're probably really nice sheets, and they'll get chocolate stains all over them, and I don't even like chocolate enough to get really nice sheets dirty. And why are you hungry when you're having sex, anyway?

You should be hungry for sex, and if you're not hungry for sex, then go eat! First, I don't want to have sex when I'm full. I'm not in the mood. Second, how can you even enjoy the food while you're busy having sex? I had a friend who didn't want to walk when she smoked; she wanted to enjoy her cigarette. I want to sit down and enjoy my food. Or I want to have sex. I don't want to do both! Plus, it's like a disguise for the sex. What are you disguising? Why are you disguising it? Food gets you to go down there without really going down there. You should enjoy—and I cringe when I say this—the taste of the other person. So if you don't want to suck on my tits without whipped cream, it's a deal breaker.

—ALEXIS

The *Seinfeld* Tap

One night I was with a guy I really *really* liked, and we were at his apartment fooling around, and then he went down on me. It was right after that episode of *Seinfeld* with "the Tap"—and I had to do the Tap because it just wasn't happening. It. Was. Not. Happening. And the next day, he was really mad at me. We were sitting at a diner, and he said, "Did you tap me?" And I was like "No! No, no, no, no, no, no! Of course not! No!"

Another time, when I was around twenty and on my semester abroad, I met this guy who was in another semester-abroad group, and we made this big plan to meet up in Germany at Oktoberfest. First, it's not that much fun to be a Jew in Germany, and second, he kept telling me how later he was going to make me scream, and he was going to do this to me and do that to me, and I was thinking, Wow, this is going to be really fun! Because back then, what did I know?

So finally we were in my hotel room, and let me tell you how *not* fun it was. I was like "A little to the left! No! A little to

Jennifer's Tips for How to Dread a Date a Little Less

- Have a "go to" outfit that *always* makes you feel great.
- Schedule a blowout. We all feel better with good hair.
- Have a mani-pedi.
- Get waxed. Or shaved. Or have laser hair removal. Hair removal always makes me feel better.
- Work out. It might sound shallow, but work from the outside in: sometimes that's way more effective than dealing from the inside out!

the right! No! There! No! Over there!" And finally I told him to stop because it was never gonna happen.

Don't tell someone what a sexual powerhouse-dynamo you are unless you really are one. As Tom Cruise's character was told in *Top Gun*: don't write checks your body can't cash!

—JENNIFER

Every Girl Has a Dating Psycho Moment

Every woman in her social romantic development has had moments when she goes crazy. Maybe you sit outside a guy's dorm waiting for him to get home, or you show up at a bar because you know he's going to be there but he doesn't know you know he's going to be there. Or you stalk his Facebook page. Or you call and hang up on him forty-seven times (this was before caller ID), thinking that by the forty-seventh call he's going to think of you and call you.

Every girl wigs out and freaks out. It's part of our genetic makeup to have that sort of turmoil over a guy at some point in our lives. It's perfectly normal, and it doesn't mean you're crazy. It just means you're vulnerable and emotional and real. And slightly psychotic. The wisest, the brightest, the most put-together women have gotten psycho over a romantic entanglement, because that's the nature of romantic entanglements.

An attraction to someone can be an addiction and an obsession. So many girls beat themselves up for being that vulnerable and that open, but it's normal. We're hardwired to be that way. But just because we're hardwired to be psychotic sometimes in relationships doesn't mean we should indulge that kind of behavior all the time or on a long-term basis. There are ways around it. Like medication. Medication is okay! If, at twenty, you need to take medicine to stop yourself from acting like a psychotic bitch, that's good. Because freaking out and thinking we can control guys and make them love us and do what we want them to *isn't* good.

When I was twenty, I was dating this guy. We hadn't even had sex—it was the sweetest, most innocent relationship, but he was about six years older than me—and I felt like he definitely took advantage of my being younger and emotionally immature. He led me on, led me on, led me on, then cut me off. And I went crazy. I got over it only after writing him like fifty thousand letters—there was no e-mail and no texting back then—but at some point he responded and roped me back in.

It was about six months later; he called out of the blue and left a message for me to call him so we could get together, and then I called him and he never called me back. That's when I really lost it. I sat outside his house and tried to get him to see me, and I went crazy. Then I finally told my brother, and my brother intervened and said I could never talk to him again and that I had to get over it. And he was right.

Now I look back on it and laugh. He was all wrong for me anyway. And it was so silly and irrational. But I think that's totally normal abnormal behavior.

—JENNIFER

You're Not the Only One Who Believes in Revenge

I think you should try to avoid harming people. Harming people isn't typically necessary. Unless they harm you. And then, be my guest. Do whatever you want. Especially to men. I think most men deserve some kind of really harsh revenge, if only to teach them a lesson that it works both ways.

I dated a guy who was always late. He didn't care if I sat at a table in a restaurant, with or without other people, for forty-five minutes, half an hour, twenty minutes—he didn't care. It

---

Alexis's Tips on How to Dump a Guy

- Get him to dump you by simply being a person he doesn't like—as expertly as you can.
- Get him to dump you by letting him see e-mails (real or fake) in which you are flirty with someone else and/or obviously cheating.
- Write a Dear John letter via e-mail (wimpy but easy).
- Give him an ultimatum: a ring or else! That should send him running for the hills. If he asks you to marry him, you can easily say no, then dump him.
- Just be honest and point out that we all want relationships to work so we can be happy, but you're sorry—this one just isn't working out.

didn't matter. Because he was busy, he was important, and he had things to do, and I wasn't and I didn't. One day, after I didn't care about him anymore, I went for drinks with someone (maybe we had sex—I can't remember) before meeting him for dinner, and I ended up unintentionally arriving about forty minutes late to meet him. He was with a bunch of people, so he wasn't sitting at the table alone, and he freaked out. And I thought, It sucks, doesn't it? I mean, it really sucks being treated like shit. He could do it, but I couldn't? Revenge is sweet, so go for it.

Given the chance now, I could really crush people. There were so many times when I should have just gotten up and walked away or just gotten in my car and driven away. A revenge-worthy deal breaker is when the guy you're with allows

Another of Alexis's Scary Dating Stories

When I was around twenty-one, I dated someone much older than I was. I'll call him Bill. One night, Bill and I were standing in line outside a movie theater, and a very attractive woman stopped by. She said hello to Bill, then looked at me and said, "Oh, is *this* the famous Alexis? Hello, Alexis. When Bill's not fucking you, he's fucking me."

Nice.

Bill's reaction to her, or lack thereof, led me to kick the windshield of his car so hard it shattered. Oops!

And guess what? That once very attractive woman now has some horrible disease that has left her face completely and permanently disfigured—like the Elephant Man.

Not that her behavior and her deformity are related, but take your anger out on the right person. If you're mad because Bill is having sex with someone else besides you, then take it out on him. Not on some girl fifteen years younger than you!

his friends or the people you're with to humiliate you and doesn't stop it. That's when you get up and walk away and you don't come back. Maybe you come back if he comes begging and admits he messed up, but otherwise you leave the room and don't go back. Don't make a scene, because you'll just look like an asshole.

I was on a date, out of town, on a weekend, with a cute boy, and we were with seven or eight of his friends who all knew one another really well and none of whom I knew at all. My mother had just gotten out of prison, and one woman (I'm assuming she didn't know who I was) went on and on about her. About what a joke and a "criminal" she was. (When I refer to my mother, I say "criminal" with quotation marks around it.) And nobody else there said anything. I was like "Really? Are you kidding me? You're just going to sit there, all of you?" My friends would never treat someone I was dating like that. It was incomprehensible.

There were many times (like that one)—before GPS—when I needed to leave wherever I was but I couldn't; I didn't know where the hell I was, and I couldn't walk or drive away no matter how much I wanted to. That's why I always say, have a way to get home from a date. If you don't know the guy well and you're going somewhere—wherever it is—have a way to get home. On your own. Don't be trapped there. Even if you think everything's going to be perfect, you should still have a way to get home if you need to.

—ALEXIS

Date without an Agenda

Dating without an agenda is going to get you where you want to go. I think men can smell an agenda. All men are relatively pathetic, so take that into account and have a good time. If you really like him and he really likes you, then there's a chance it'll work. Of course, there's also a chance it won't. I know plenty of girls who have gone out with bad boys, and then they finally decide to go out with a "nice guy," and the nice guy ends up shooting heroin and leaving her for a woman he met online. There's no answer.

Being single has never been a huge issue for me, and in fact it's probably a bigger issue for everyone else. I've never felt odd around couples. It would be annoying if I could tell that they were worried about me, because obviously they don't need to be. I don't get all upset about

You're Not the Only One Who Thinks Breaking Up in an E-mail Is Okay (Sometimes)

Alexis: How many times have you been dumped?

Jennifer: A couple. But not a lot. One was "constructive dumping," because I found out he had a girlfriend. Nowadays people break up in texts or e-mails. It's no longer the Call or the Dinner.

Alexis: Some people find that really offensive, but I don't. I went out with someone on one or two dates and I sent him an e-mail that said, "It's just not working for me." And he wrote back that he really would've appreciated a phone call. And what would the phone call have done? Given him a chance to try to convince me to change my mind or embarrass me?

Jennifer: I have a problem with two- or three-year relationships and a breakup e-mail. But it's fine if it's an early-on situation. If you've gone out only once or twice, it's not really breaking up, it's just saying, "Let's not waste our time."

Alexis: So after a two- or three-year relationship you don't want to just get an e-mail?

Jennifer: No. That's wrong. Unless what's written is the most beautiful loving note that spares the person's feelings. The "It's not you, it's me" note. And that e-mail can serve as a way to mitigate the embarrassment of being dumped. The dumped person can share that note with all of her friends and loved ones and say, "Look! He loved me, but it just wasn't right. Right now. With me."

being single—I don't want to be the center of attention in that way. If people find you pitiable, that sucks. Nobody wants to be pitied. And why should you be? If you were a man, you'd just be a "player."

—ALEXIS

You're Not Defective. You're Just Defective for That Particular Person

Alexis taught me this: If he doesn't like you, then he's not the right guy for *you*. So if you're too needy for him, it's just that *you're* too needy for *him*. You shouldn't think you're defective. It's more like you're defective for *that guy*. I found someone who needs me as much as I need him, which is amazing. But there were plenty of people who found me annoying. There were plenty of guys I wasn't remotely right for, and they would never have given me what I wanted, but I wanted them *because* they weren't giving me what I wanted. Ultimately they never would have made me happy. So I framed it in my head that *I* was the loser, but really there were no losers, just two incompatible people.

So if you can, stop being ashamed and stop thinking that there's something wrong with you. Chances are, if he asked you out in the first place, he thought you were pretty enough or thin enough. When I revisit what I went through—the crushes that really mattered—what was so screwy with me was I always thought if I could just get someone to be attracted to me, then he'd fall in love with me. So when he didn't fall in love with me, I didn't understand why. I thought it was easy to love me but not so easy to want to have sex with me. I wasn't one of those girls who had that kind of confidence, so I didn't put it out there—I didn't express myself in a comfortable manner because I felt so weird about it. I had so much self-loathing about my whole body that I didn't think anyone could possibly desire me in that way.

—JENNIFER

Flirting? We love flirting! Even though we're both over-forty MILF types at this point and there's never anyone to flirt with at our office—*ever*—we think flirting keeps you young and that it can be good, clean fun. As long as you don't get crazy. And as long as you don't let the person you're dating get crazy, either.

- *It's okay if your boyfriend flirts with someone else, as long as he doesn't do it right in front of you.* If I don't know you're flirting with someone else, I don't care. If it's just a sport, I guess I don't have a problem with it. I don't want to have to watch it—and I don't want you to have sex with her—but if you want to flirt with her for entertainment, fine.

- *It's also okay if your boyfriend flirts with someone else as long as he doesn't mess with her head.* Don't hurt somebody else for no reason. Don't flirt with her if it's going to make her miserable. That's no good. Flirting is one thing; messing with someone's head is something else entirely. Making a person think that there's a possibility when there isn't one? It's just mean. Get over it. Stop it. Don't lead her on to the point where she thinks she's really going to get something. And don't lead him on unless you hate him for some reason—like, because he's male, which would be a good enough reason for me, and no doubt he's done the same thing to a million other girls. Then if you want to punish him, go ahead. I don't care.

- *If he does flirt right in front of you: walk out.* Leave. You really have to have the balls to get up and walk away. Literally, go

**Alexis's Rules
for Flirting**

home. Go home and don't answer the phone for a day. And if he really likes you and isn't going to do it again, he'll keep trying to get in touch with you. Otherwise, you're involved with someone who doesn't like you enough. Or, at the very least, he likes the other person more. Whatever. It doesn't matter. Eitherz way, something unpleasant is going to happen. If being dissed wasn't enough for you, something worse will happen.

You have to know that this is a line that can't be crossed, and you have to be ready for something like that to happen in your life. Because it's a hard thing to do—to be ready to do what you need to do. Your parents, your friends—they should tell you that you're dating a dick. And if they do? And if you are? Walk away. Because the point is that you're never going to get what you want from this person. Never. It's not even about how hard it is to walk away. Because you're going to be made miserable day after day after day with this person. It's just about how long he allows you to stay around, like a cat playing with a mouse until it's too maimed to move or it kills it.

Fun Things to Do with Your Panties When You're on a Date

A fun thing to do at dinner when you're first dating is to go to the bathroom and then come back with your panties around your wrist. Then you hand them to the guy.

—ALEXIS

Even better is when you're sitting at the table and you actually *remove* your panties while *at* the table and then hand them to him *under* the table.

—JENNIFER

Just because Alexis and Jennifer talk about sex all the time and have very strong opinions about sex—from stripper poles to guys who talk during sex to people who can't shut up about their sex lives—that doesn't mean they grew up talking about it at home. In fact, almost everything they learned about sex they didn't learn from their parents.

What Jennifer's Mother Said When She Asked Her What Sixty-Nine Was

I remember that when I was seven years old, I asked my mother what sixty-nine was, because I'd asked my brother and my sister and they didn't want to tell me. So they said, "Ask Mommy." So I did. And she said, "It's when a man and a woman kiss each other's genitals." Yeah, I was not comfortable with that response.

—JENNIFER

Alexis Didn't Have to Ask Her Parents about Sex Because She Already Knew Everything

I think I was such a precocious reader that nothing was ever a surprise to me. That and the fact that my parents had the annoying habit of taking me to more than my fair share of R-rated films, anyway. When I was really young, they took me to a movie where at some point in the film everyone was doing a maypole around some guy's penis that's the size of a house—literally. I think the movie was Ken Russell's *Lisztomania*—

described by the Internet Movie Database as "a send-up of the bawdy life of Romantic composer/piano virtuoso Franz Liszt, with ubiquitous phallic imagery and a good portion of the film devoted to Liszt's 'friendship' with fellow composer Richard Wagner," starring Roger Daltrey. I was ten. Then my parents walked out. I thought, It's kinda late!

—ALEXIS

Guys Who Talk during Sex Are Annoying Liars

I went through most of my life really hating when guys talked during sex. I would just be quiet, so there wasn't a lot of talking. Ever. And I think as you get older, maybe it becomes less of a no-no. Maybe you become more adventurous, or bored, or maybe it just depends on the person you're with. But lately, if someone tells me I'm hot while we're having sex, it ruins it for me.

I'm hot? Why are you telling me this now? We're already in bed! We're already having sex! You're already getting what you want! I'm getting what I want. But what I don't want at this very moment is to be lied to, because it's annoying and I don't believe you. I've become completely and bizarrely para- noid—I'm here already! Shut up! I'm here! You are inside me! Shut up! You want to talk about something else? Okay! But I don't want to hear any lies right at this moment. I'm not inter- ested. If you want me to lie to you about something, I can do that. As long as it's out in the open that it's a lie. In fact, I might ask you to lie to me.

Now I understand why men shtup hookers. Because some- times you just want that lie, but somehow, knowing it's a lie makes it okay.

—ALEXIS

You're Not the Only One Who Dated Someone Who Would Not Go into Your Pants

I'm not sure if I can really even call it dating, but we spent inordinate amounts of time on the phone and texting and e-mailing. I mean, *in-or-di-nate*. Hours and hours and hours a day, sometimes. Then, after two or three months of this, he finally said, "I'm just not attracted to you."

—ALEXIS

There's Something Wrong with You If You Can't Shut Up about Your Sex Life

Someone tells you she's pregnant, but she doesn't want everyone to know, and five minutes later you announce it in front of a hundred people. What's your problem that you can't respect her privacy? What's wrong with you that you can't shut up? You need to examine yourself, because it's your problem that you can't be quiet. If you have a compulsion to tell—even when it's in your best interest to just shut up—then you need to look at that. It goes along with the compulsion to be the first one to tell bad news, like when somebody famous dies.

The worst is when you talk about people you've had sex with. Saying you had sex with so-and-so is fine. You can tell detailed stories to friends, but in that case, names should never be used. It's just not nice, it's nobody's business, and it's creepy. Because then you can't have any fun in bed. You can say that sex was good or bad, that you liked having sex with someone or you didn't, but it shouldn't go any further than that, because then it's gross and hurtful.

Someone I know once complained that a guy she had dated wanted her to call him Daddy. Why would you tell that to people he knows? I mean, if you're going to tell, tell strangers. But *you* were the one there calling him Daddy, so who's the weirdo? You're just as weird as he is!

—ALEXIS

There's Only One Reason to Have a Stripper Pole in Your Bedroom

Women pole-dancing for a living is very different from women pole-dancing for their husbands or boyfriends. The fact that men don't have to do anything like that for us really pisses me off.

I also don't like the fact that people install poles in their bedrooms. The only reason to have a stripper pole in your bedroom is if you need something to put the handcuffs around.

—ALEXIS

For Those of You Taking Notes at Home: Clinical Terms for All of Your Relationship Phobias

Fear of staying single	anuptaphobia
Fear of being touched	aphenphosmphobia
Fear of men	arrhenphobia
Fear of women	gynephobia
Fear of beautiful women	caligynephobia
Fear of the opposite sex	heterophobia
Fear of dancing	chorophobia
Fear of coitus	coitophobia
Fear of undressing in front of someone	dishabiliophobia
Fear of sexual love	erotophobia
Fear of female genitalia	eurotophobia
Fear of marriage	gamophobia
Fear of sex	genophobia
Fear of nudity	gymnophobia
Fear of bald people	peladophobia
Fear of becoming bald	phalacrophobia
Fear of kissing	philemaphobia

And then, there's guy-crying in relationships. We don't understand. Is there a question here?

There should be no guy-crying in relationships. And if there is guy-crying, there better be a really good reason for it. Crying during a TV commercial isn't a good reason. Crying during a fight isn't a good reason, either. Crying during a movie, once in a while, might be okay, but if a guy is guy-crying all the time over everything? Please. We can't deal with it.

- Having the divorce talk. The divorce talk is the only time that guy-crying is truly justified. And even then, it would be nice if he could keep his man-tears to himself.

- If his dog dies, he can cry. But *not* if his cat dies. Ever.

- If he finds you having sex with his best friend, then he can cry.

Then there are guys who don't like animals. Or who say they love animals but actually hate them. This is a big problem for us. We'd even go so far as to say it's a deal breaker.

Guys Who Say They Love Dogs but Are Too Afraid to Touch Your Bulldogs Are Pussies

Often when I dated a guy while I had two bulldogs, he'd say, "I love dogs!" Really? Then why don't you *touch* them, you freak? Why are your arms crossed protectively over your chest? One guy wouldn't get out of the car the first time he came over because he was "afraid of the dogs." As if I'd invite you over and leave my vicious, man-eating dogs in the yard to greet you.

Guys who are afraid of dogs might be pussies, but guys with cats—plural—are weird. Cats smell. And the whole litter box situation is just not right. I mean, come on. Especially if you have a small house or apartment. If I met a guy and he had cats—plural—that would scare me.

—ALEXIS

Alexis's first bulldog, Homer.

Guys Who Hate Animals Are the Worst

Worse than a guy with cats is a guy who hates all animals. How can you automatically dislike a defenseless, innocent, guileless animal? I understand a distaste for human beings, but a distaste for animals? That makes me think there's something wrong with him. I *love* animals. Part of me wanted to be a vet when I was a kid, but I couldn't handle the science and the dying or the animal parts. I just wanted to play with the puppies.

That was one of the ways I knew that my husband was a good guy, because when he first came to my apartment, he walked in the door; saw my dog, a standard poodle—her name was Annabelle; and went right over to her. He loved her. And she loved him! My husband grew up with a standard poodle and so he got it.

—JENNIFER

1. *If you're unhappy, it might be because he doesn't like you enough.* It's that simple. If you're unhappy, he might like you, but he doesn't like you *enough*.

2. *You can't argue someone into liking you.* You think you can, but you're desperate and you're a little out of your mind. You're a little upset, you're a little hysterical, but you can't make him like you. It would be nice if someone at some point in your life had told you this; it would be nice, for instance, if your mother was with-it enough to say, "This is going to happen, so be ready for it." But unfortunately, nobody tells you that. You have to learn it for yourself—that it's not you. It's just that *you're* not right for *him*.

3. *Not everybody likes everybody.* And there's nothing you can do about it. Whatever it is about you, you can't change it. So don't even try.

4. *There's someone for everyone.* People like to say things like "Oh, I don't want a guy who's clingy" or "I need a guy who gives me a lot of attention." But all it really boils down to is whether you like him. Because if you like the guy—if you like the guy *enough*—you're happy he called you from a business trip or from his paintball-bonanza weekend. But if you're not into him and he calls you from the paintball-bonanza weekend, you're thinking, God, what a *loser*! So again, it's not that there's something wrong with you—it's just that most women go straight to that place in their minds. Even though there might indeed be something wrong with you, there's someone out there who won't mind. You just have to find him.

The Most Important Dating and Relationship Advice Alexis and Jennifer Want to Leave You With (Seriously)

5. *The reason he doesn't like you usually isn't the reason you think.* It's not because of your thighs. Or your stomach. It's because there's no chemistry. Stop trying to make sparks fly where none ever will. Move on. Because there's someone out there who's going to like you—and even love you—just the way you are.

Jennifer wishes that she'd known Alexis when she was younger and still dating, because she wasted so much time and energy on guys who didn't like her enough. "They might have liked me, and they may have wanted to have sex with me, but they didn't love me, and they were never going to be good to me. And it was never going to be right. But I thought that being abrasive or being in their face would make them want me, which was absurd." People have a very hard time giving tough love—to tell you to stop—but you have to stop. Because you're not going to get what you want from someone who doesn't like you or love you enough. That's the key.

Alexis and Jennifer's Dating Deal Breakers (in No Particular Order)

- *Liars.* Dating a liar is not okay.

- *Cheapskates.* It doesn't matter how much a guy spends on you, but he can't be cheap.

- *Cadillac sedans.* Deal breaker.

- *A Chrysler LeBaron.* Deal breaker.

- *A yellow Ferrari.* Deal breaker.

- *A red Ferrari.* Deal breaker.

- *A black Ferrari.* Really close to being a deal breaker. (Some Ferraris are okay: the California and the 599 GTB.)

- *A Lotus.* Deal breaker.

- *Guys with ponytails.* Deal breaker.

- *Mostly bald guys with ponytails.* The biggest deal breaker on the entire planet. We don't care how much hair you have—we don't like a ponytail under any circumstances. Why do you have a ponytail? *Why?*

- *Guys who wear skinny jeans.* If a guy is wearing skinny jeans, he better be a rock star or gay. If you're punky and that's your style, great. But if it isn't, what are you doing?

- *Womanly hips on a man.* It's just absolutely unacceptable. *Get thee to a gym.* We know it's something you're born with, but build up your shoulders. Do something. Because it's terrible. Alexis once dated a guy with a woman's belly. "It made me insane. I couldn't believe he allowed himself to be that way. He had a belly, like a girl!"

- *Men with long hair.* It's gross. And the hair's all broken and they don't know how to take care of it, and if they did, that would be even worse. Imagine a guy with really long hair that was smooth and blow-dried, brushed back into a nice ponytail. OMG. Cut your hair. Cut. Your. Hair.

- *Men who can't deal with the fact that they're losing their hair.* You either have it or you don't, and you better not let us know that you have to work on it. We don't want to see you with a brush and a curling iron. That curling iron better be up your ass and not in your hair, because it's a total deal breaker. We know a lot of men have to work on it, but we don't want to know about it. And we really prefer if you didn't have to. Find a shampoo that makes it so that you don't have to blow-dry your hair, or cut your hair shorter.

    We like guys with hair, but Alexis *loves* a crew cut. "I *love* it. A guy who looks good with a crew cut is hot. I like the military thing."

    And don't get plugs. Just deal with it. Or if you're going to get plugs, start early. And find the best person in the world to do it—hair by hair—and start weaving before your hair is falling out. But don't just appear—after years of being almost cue-ball bald—with black hair on the top of your head and pretend that it's not new. It's shocking! We've known men who were bald for years and then one day they show up with hair on their heads. It's weird! If you know you're going to lose your hair, shave your head when you're young. Ask one of your best friends, "Should I start fixing this now, or am I going to look okay bald?" But you have to deal with it, because, in the end, women really don't care. They just don't.

- *Men who name their penises.* Beyond deal breaker.

- Fussy metrosexual types. We don't want to know that you're fussy with your hair. Because we don't like that in a guy. We don't want to be getting dressed and fighting over the hair dryer and the round brush.

- *Pretentious self-conscious hipster facial hair.* Deal breaker. Any guy who takes himself too seriously and has stupid facial hair is annoying. But if you're going to have facial hair, keep it clean.

- *Mutton chops or a handlebar mustache.* We don't know who you are or where you're coming from, but go back to the swamps and stay away from us. Maybe it has to do with where we live, maybe it's a location thing or a cultural thing, but it's weird, and we don't get it. A total deal breaker.

- *Nose hair.* Get rid of it. You have boogers in your nose because you have hair there to hold them in. Please don't make us look at your nose hair. It's distracting and disgusting. And why isn't someone in your life telling you to do something about it?

- *Weird stray hairs.* We don't even like that weird stray hair in the middle of your cheek that you never remember to shave. That makes us want to hurl. Hurl! Alexis dated a guy who now apparently has a beard down to his belly because that's how it grows, but WTF is he doing? He just wants attention in the weirdest way. He wants attention and it's all under the guise of not wanting any attention.

- *Piercings and tattoos.* What's your problem? What is it? What's that on your face? The worst is the giant earplugs that make your earlobe split open. And what about boogers when you have a nose ring? You can't get rid of the holes made by piercings, people. They're permanent (or they're going to last for a really long time). You're really sure you're going to want that Chinese symbol on your body twenty years from now? You don't even know what the symbol means! If you really want to be special, don't do what everybody else is doing. How about being so special that you don't have a goddamn tattoo? Because you can't change your mind. Getting piercings and tattoos isn't like dyeing your hair blue. One or two earrings on a guy is okay, but there's something about the symmetry of one earring in each earlobe on a guy that's off-putting.

- *White shoes.* And white Dockers. Total deal breakers.

- *Not owning sneakers.* Strange and gross. One guy Jennifer dated didn't own a pair of sneakers. They had two dates, and he told her on the second date that he didn't have sneakers. It was such a turnoff! There was something bizarre about the idea that he wouldn't need a pair of sneakers or wouldn't *want* a pair of sneakers! Run around! Play ball! Jennifer found it creepy and a total deal breaker.

6

Wrapping Your Own Christmas Presents

Alexis and Jennifer on Growing Up Dysfunctional

The party was always at my house.

Jennifer Koppelman Hutt

~

The party was never at my house.

Alexis Stewart

Oy, family and childhood. Where to begin? How about with this obvious fact: Alexis and Jennifer both had completely abnormal childhoods.

Everyone's family is crazy is in its own way; no one has perfect parents or grows up unscathed and not needing intensive psychotherapy. But our families and childhoods were particularly crazy and imperfect. Jennifer's parents smothered her to the point of making her phobic about everything and needing to have human contact—by phone, by text, by e-mail, in person—every minute of every day. Alexis's parents left her alone so much that she basically hates to be around people. She needs tons of space. But we do have one thing in common in the way we were raised: we both grew up in situations where we didn't have to kiss anybody's ass.

Everybody knows Alexis's background, but Alexis doesn't think that everyone knows the level of privilege and fanciness Jennifer was raised with. When Jennifer was younger, her father was in the music business. She went on vacation with people like Barbra Streisand, and Run-DMC and the Beastie Boys performed at her sweet sixteen party. (Bubbles, Michael Jackson's chimp, was also in attendance.) She lived in a house designed by the same architect who designed the Boston Public Library, the second Madison Square Garden, and one of the Newport mansions, and she never went anywhere without a limousine because her parents were afraid she'd be kidnapped. So even though our stories are so opposite it sounds like we came from different planets, the result is the same: we're both freaks!

I Was Shamed into Never Picking My Nose Again

I was eight, maybe nine, and I was in a car with Barbra Streisand and her then husband, Jon Peters—the notorious Hollywood hairdresser, now a producer, who was immortalized by Warren Beatty in the movie *Shampoo*—and a bunch of other people. I think we were driving through Malibu, but it doesn't matter. All that matters is that I was sitting in the backseat, and at some point I stuck my finger in my nose and Jon saw me. He said something like "Pick a winner!" I was mortified. I'm not sure if anyone else heard what he said, but it didn't matter. I never picked my nose in public again.

—JENNIFER

Jenny with movie producer Jon Peters.

My Mother Picked Me Up from School Dressed Like Martha Stewart Because She *Was* Martha Stewart

Do you know how mortified I was by my mother's outfits when I was in grade school? She would come to my school in clogs and an apron. I thought it was the *most* embarrassing thing ever when I was in fourth or fifth grade and I'd see her walking down the hall to pick me up for a dentist appointment. I'd just be horrified and ask, "What are you wearing?!" She'd just look at me and say, "Shut up and get in the car."

—ALEXIS

Bare-bottomed Alexis in front of the house in Massachusetts.

You're Probably the Only One Whose Mother Is Good at Everything Like Martha Stewart Because She *Is* Martha Stewart

Martha does everything better! You can't win!

I grew up with a glue gun pointed at my head. You know what would happen if I didn't pay attention? If I didn't do something perfectly, I had to do it again. So I learned quickly.

—ALEXIS

My Mother Brought Me Lederhosen from Her Trip Abroad

My mother went to Switzerland when I was a little kid, and she came home not with a box of chocolates but with a *pair of lederhosen.* For a seven- or eight-year-old! I said, "You *want* me to be stoned to death at school?"

—ALEXIS

The Lunch-Box Problem

I wasn't allowed to have a lunch box. I was given a little insulated box from the Irongate Caviar Company.

—ALEXIS

I had every kitschy lunch box imaginable.

—JENNIFER

More from the Larry King Interview

Larry King: Your mother has said of herself, "My life is my work, and my work is my life." Where does that include Alexis?

Alexis Stewart: Well, luckily, her work is pretty interesting, so it's not not-fun to be involved in it.

King: So she was involved in your life.

Stewart: Absolutely, very involved. I would beg her to be less involved.

King: Are you close with your dad?

Stewart: No, no, I'm not close.

King: That's sad. Daddies and daughters are usually close.

Stewart: Are they? I think there are plenty of daddies and daughters that aren't close.

My Mother Would *Forget* to Pick Me Up at the End of the Day

My mother would often forget to pick me up. Five hours later I'd have to call someone else's mother from the Hunt Club, where I went horseback riding, and by then it was dark and I'd been waiting for hours for someone to come get me, and nobody ever did. My mother would pull in at exactly the same time as my friend's mother whom I'd called, and she was beyond apologetic, but I think it was more about being embarrassed. Keeping me waiting didn't bother her. And I don't think it would have bothered me so much except that it was getting cold and I was really bored. I don't remember being scared. I just remember being a little mortified that I had to call someone else and cause her any kind of inconvenience.

—ALEXIS

Jenny with her sister, Stacy, and her mother, Bunny.

You Have to Get Over the Mistakes Your Parents Made

People shouldn't spend their whole lives moaning about every single mistake their parents made. Our parents made mistakes raising us, and we'll make mistakes raising our kids, too. That's life. At some point you have to get on with it. You know what's wrong with you, and you know what's wrong with them, and while it doesn't mean that you don't have lingering emotional issues, you have to move forward; otherwise it'll rule your life. I don't think my family was or is perfect at all. I'm about acceptance. I like most of my family most of the time. I have issues, but I choose not to dwell on them.

—JENNIFER

My Parents Ruined My Life

I know I should get over it (I'm an adult, or so they say), but still! I'll probably never stop wishing that I could change whether my parents moved out of New York City. That was a defining event for me. I mean, growing up in Connecticut? What was fun about that? I was in the most interesting city in the world, and they put me in the least interesting state on the planet. Great.

My parents never really separated from New York, but I was forced to. They had their commuting friends—my mother wanted a farm, but I'd rather it had been in Vermont than Connecticut. It was right in between city and farm—it wasn't rural enough, and it wasn't cosmopolitan enough. It was preppy. And that just didn't work for me. Plus, they weren't willing to support the preppy lifestyle, so I felt like an outcast since I didn't have all of the clothes and trappings that everyone else had.

Martha was one of six kids—she didn't have anything growing up—which is probably why she parented the way she did. (And when I say "parented," I use the term very loosely, as in a very hands-off approach to child rearing.) There are lots of studies about the "new" parenting: how children now don't know how to do normal chores like laundry or loading a dishwasher or making their beds because their parents want them doing exotic things to get into college. Clearly, the hovering-helicopter-soccer-mom parenting style isn't great, but our parents' generation didn't think at all about what they were doing.

Mirror Wisdom

If you look in the mirror and you see your mother, change!

—ALEXIS

I'm sick of hearing that our parents did the best they could. You mean, without thought? It wasn't the best they could do: it's just what they did *without thinking about it*. They barely considered what effect their behavior or decisions would have on us. Jennifer's parents were chauffeuring her all around town and wouldn't let her go anywhere without a limousine, and my parents were sending me out to the corner at ten to wait for a taxi all by myself in the middle of the night in the middle of nowhere.

Everybody always wants to know what it's like to have Martha Stewart as a mother. Every reporter who's ever written about my mother or about me writes about what a bad relationship we have. It's so boring. And it's not true. Every mother and daughter relationship is complicated. Ours is just lived out in public and appears one-dimensional.

Of course my mother is difficult. Everybody knows that. I'm difficult, too. But we're close in many ways. People like to think that Martha didn't pay attention to me. It's just not true. The stories I tell about my childhood are all true. Of *course* they're true. I couldn't make this stuff up. *Nobody* could. (Okay, maybe I exaggerate a little bit.) And my mother doesn't deny any of it.

—ALEXIS

It's True—I Can Hold a Grudge Forever

When I was eight years old my mother took my clear umbrella to New York and lost it. It was devastating—and emotionally scarring. I didn't have a lot of stuff. My parents weren't going to spend money on "stuff." My mother never got me another one. She didn't care. I loved my umbrella, and then I had nothing. And no one gave me anything to replace it—there was no consolation prize. Now I don't want anyone touching my clear umbrella. You can't have it, you can't borrow it, and you can't look through it—just leave it alone. It's *my* umbrella.

—ALEXIS

I Am So-o-o Tired of Being Asked to Become a Different Person (Hello—It's Too Late!)

My parents blame me for my personality, but they're the ones who made me that way. My mother hates that I'm shy. She can't stand that I like to be alone. I don't know if I love it, either, but I do like to be alone. I don't complain about it. But it often gets in the way of the outgoing person she wishes I was. It's deeply ironic, since she and my father taught me to be that way—or made it so I didn't know I had an option of being any other way.

Oh, sorry! You don't like that I like being by myself? That interferes with your idea of who I should be? Really? Maybe you shouldn't have moved me at a very impressionable age to a town where I knew no one, where I spent the entire summer alone and then went to a new school. I was a very outgoing kid with a lot of friends when I lived in New York. It was fun there: there were kids my age in the building, there were kids my age a block away, and it was great.

But then you whipped me out of there and put me, basically, in a goddamn wilderness (if you can call two-acre zoning "wilderness"). I had no friends. I had nothing. And then I became incredibly introverted. I don't know if I would've ended up this way anyway—but chances are, our move had a huge effect on me. It changed me. I went from being incredibly bossy and trying to take over my pre-K class to never talking. And you don't think *maybe* your decision to move had anything to do with it? You should be glad I was so comfortable being alone. If I hadn't been, it would have been a big pain in the ass for you because I would have been constantly freaking out.

—ALEXIS

My Family Message Was "You're Great, Except You're *Fat*"

My childhood was different: Lots of limousines. Lots of people. Lots of parental involvement. Independence was fostered as long as there was a bodyguard or someone to protect me while I was being independent. The message to me was: you can do anything you want to do; you're great, except you're fat.

—JENNIFER

My Mother Sent Me Spelling Lists at Sleepaway Camp Instead of Care Packages

When I went to sleepaway camp, my mother did not send me off with a whole survival kit like the one she made for some

A letter from Martha to Alexis at camp.

poor boy on one of her shows. I was never given anything to take to camp, only the bare minimum. She sent me off with a stack of stamped-and-addressed postcards. I barely used them, because when I did, she answered them with lists of words I needed to learn how to spell.

—ALEXIS

My Parents Wouldn't Play Board Games with Me Even Though I Had No One Else to Play Them With

There wasn't a lot of board-game playing in my house. First of all, the games were considered too expensive. I played Monopoly, but our set was secondhand, and there were pieces missing. In addition, my parents didn't have that much free time or patience for entertaining children. And then there was just me—six miles away from my nearest friend. There was a game called Mastermind where you had to figure out a code with little clues—it was aesthetically horrible, in retrospect, this brown plastic thing—so my parents would play a few times with me and then they'd be like, "Okay, now you can play by yourself." But you couldn't play it by yourself! So it was "Go read a book!"

—ALEXIS

Martha on Alexis

She's an only child who was always treated as an adult, basically. And I think that may be great and it may be horrible. We don't know for sure. But she learned everything. She's a very accomplished young woman. She knows everything. She's much smarter than I am, too, in her way. And she's just extremely opinionated, which is great for a television personality. And she is a perfectionist in her way. She's my daughter.

My Mother Gave Me a Bell to Ring When I Was Home Sick, but She Didn't Answer It

I would get the flu approximately once a year, if that often, and maybe be home for five days from school. One time my mother gave me a bell to ring if I needed her, because I got a sore throat and couldn't speak. So I was really thirsty and I rang the bell for about four hours. When she finally came up the stairs, she said, "I heard that ringing and ringing, and I didn't know what it was!" It's true. She'll admit it. She didn't know what the ringing was. She was working. She had stuff to do. I survived. Sort of.

—ALEXIS

Martha as Grandmother

Alexis: My mother always says, "Alexis, I just want you to be happy." But what she really means is "I want you to be happy. *As long as it's on my terms.*"

Jennifer: Does she like little children?

Alexis: I'm not sure. She didn't like me. But then again, not many people do like me.

Jennifer: Actually, in real life she does like kids. She's great with mine. She once took my daughter and my nieces to *Hannah Montana.* Are you shocked?

Alexis: I am shocked! Do you think my mother will allow my daughter to have toys?

Jennifer: Yes. I think your mother will be a doting grandmother and shower her with thousands of toys.

Alexis: And all the love I never got?

Jennifer: Yes! It'll be a do-over!

I Envied Other People's Families because They Encouraged Their Kids to Eat

I didn't ever want to have someone else's family, but I did want to hang out at other people's houses. It was mostly because my mother was so screwy about food. At my friend Leslie's house, for instance, I felt like the parents encouraged her to eat. That was odd to me. They also weren't overly involved with their kids. My parents were *so* involved, so I kind of welcomed that small bit of breathing room.

But then there were other houses where I'd never want to be. My other friend's parents were so strict with her I couldn't understand it. They were strict with where she was going and who she was hanging with—she was the first child—and they were like drill sergeants. That's what it felt like. Then I had another friend whose parents gave her so much freedom and independence that I found it scary. So there has to be a balance between support and smothering, between independence and neglect.

—JENNIFER

I Never Had a Themed Birthday Party

Where were *my* themed birthday parties? My birthday parties *sucked*. I never even had cupcakes. I wasn't allowed to have anything. I never had a pretty party. My mother would be like "Oops, I forgot it was your birthday. Here's a pound cake. Here's a pillar candle. Let's shove it in the center of the pound cake and bob for apples. That's fun!"

—ALEXIS

The cathartic sharing has been nonstop, we know. Time for a breather. Is this truly the first part of the chapter where some pleasant stories are going to be shared?

My Sweet Sixteen Party

My parents surprised me by hiring Run-DMC and the Beastie Boys. I had written my sweet sixteen invitation, a rap song sent out on a cassette tape (it was 1986) to the tune of "You Talk Too Much" by Run-DMC, so my parents hired the group to perform. It was really wild. Alexis can't believe people had to listen to the whole thing, but they loved it so much that they took it with them over the summer and played it for all their friends at camp and on their teen tours.

—JENNIFER

Hey kids over there you know
*   it's 'bout that time*
And if you don't know what
*   I mean then it's sure a crime.*
If you look at the date
and then you look a bit more
you'll be able to see
just what's in store.
This might be a hint
I say
Your tie should be black . . .
And girls will wear gowns.
Hey that's a fact
My sweet sixteen
You'll soon hear the date
My sweet sixteen
Oh boy I really can't wait.
May the 10th's the date
Please don't look a mess
Eight o'clock is the time
Black tie is the dress
_____ is the number
_____ is the street
_____ is the town
This is where we will meet
My sweet sixteen

You now know the date
My sweet sixteen
Get psyched it's gonna be
*   great*
Respondez s'il vous plait
That's RSVP
You'll be glad that you did
Just you wait and see
Pick up the phone
And dial for me
516-000-0000
My sweet sixteen
You now know it all
My sweet sixteen
It'll be such a ball
You'll hear lots of music
Both disco and rock
And so many surprises
It'll be a shock
We'll have so much fun . . .
*   it'll be a blast*
So RSVP and don't be last
My sweet sixteen
Call me right now
My sweet sixteen
It'll be such a wow!

The Party Was Always at My House

The party was always at my house, in the kitchen. Our house was always the house everybody hung out in. It was always filled with kids: my friends and my siblings' friends. And there was no off-limits space in the house. Everyone was everywhere. My friends would go into my parents' bedroom and sit on the bed with my mother. They were all friends with her and they all adored her, but they also knew she was nutty and totally eccentric and would commiserate with me when she drove me crazy. Everybody knew how much she loved me to the point of smothering—and that her limitations were caused by her issues.

—JENNIFER

I Didn't Have Chores, and We Paid People to Do Crafts and Cook

There wasn't a lot of cooking and crafting going on in my house. We had a housekeeper. We paid for people to cook and do crafts with us. I didn't have chores, but I wasn't allowed to throw clothes around my room or make a giant mess and just walk away. I liked cleaning our kitchen (more food to sneak!). I wasn't allowed to be disrespectful, gross, or entitled. My mother would have thought that was disgusting. And if we stayed in a hotel, I couldn't leave the room like a pigsty.

—JENNIFER

Wow, the good was so short-lived! And incredibly, it all came from Jennifer. There are more good stories coming, but until then, we're going back to our regularly scheduled, completely justified, and wholly entertaining complaining.

The Party Was Never at My House

The party was never at my house. Sorry—once it was, and we had bobbing for apples as one of the "games." It's a miracle I had even a single friend growing up.

There was never anything to eat at my house. Other people had food. I had no food. My friends lived in the nicest fanciest houses ever—with elevators and walk-in refrigerators—and they might have thought I was interesting enough, but in the end I don't think they thought it was particularly interesting to come to my house. It was just odd. And uncomfortable. The house was physically uncomfortable—unbelievably physically uncomfortable, and there might have been screaming between me and my mother—and there was no food. There were ingredients but no prepared food of any kind.

One summer weekend I invited some kids over, and my mother took us to Massachusetts—it was a hundred degrees and she made us rake formerly knee-high grass that had just been cut. These were kids who didn't even know what a rake was. Good times, right? We drove four hours so they could rake? Thanks, Mom! I didn't have people over because they were going to have to do something like clean out the chicken coop. So I'd try to go to other people's houses.

—ALEXIS

When I Was Growing Up, My Mother Barely Remembered Halloween Existed

My mother gets so into Halloween that it's amazing she could never remember it existed when I was a child. She did make one good costume, though: a giant pink rabbit. But I had to wear loafers with it. Mortifying. And I had to use it three years in a row.

She never had candy for Halloween when I was growing up. None. Let me tell you: there were no fluorescent wristbands. There were no costumes. There was no anything. We turned off all the lights and pretended we weren't home, and my mother never had anything but apples and pennies to annoy the children with. Now she's obsessed with Halloween: The books. The television specials. The costumes. The "body parts" and "brains" floating in jars of colored water, the "severed finger" cookies. Martha likes to scare adults and kids alike. Scaring kids is fine with me; it's scaring the adults that I don't get.

My parents actually, once or twice, went all out with the Easter basket. Once or twice. One year I woke up, and right next to me there was this giant basket filled with Perugina. I know, most kids want a cheap chocolate bunny and Cadbury Crème eggs, but I didn't. I liked hazelnuts. I still do. I loved that basket.

—ALEXIS

Everyone Thinks I Grew Up in a Palace Eating Bonbons

I had tons of chores, although they weren't labeled as such. The idea that taking out the garbage is something that kids grumble about is bizarre to me. I always made the bed, took the trash out, cleaned, cooked, did the dishes, fed the dog, fed the goats, and fed the chickens and cleaned out their coop. Maybe my anal-compulsiveness made these things easy for me, because I usually didn't question what I had to do. But even though I did all that work, I wasn't even given an allowance every week or month the way other kids were. I would steal the change my father left on the dresser every night.

It would have been nice if I didn't need to do that, but that was the only way I could buy something to eat after school if I wasn't going directly home. Did there come a point in my life when my mother's success made my financial life enviable in most people's eyes? Sure. But people know nothing about when, how much, or any of the other circumstances involved. They want to be angry, so they just assume that I grew up being waited on hand and foot.

Everybody always asks me about being an only child, and I never know what to say. I don't know what it would have been like to have siblings or how it would have changed me. I imagine that it would have changed me, but I have no idea how. I hate sharing a bedroom. I hate sharing my stuff. It doesn't mean I'm not generous. I just don't want people rifling through my things. But I think that could happen because you have siblings, too, not just because you don't have siblings.

—ALEXIS

Martha on Being a Working Mother

When I got married and had a child and went to work, my day was all day, all night. You lose your sense of balance. That was in the late '60s, '70s, women went to work, they went crazy. They thought the workplace was much more exciting than the home. They thought the family could wait. And you know what? The family can't wait. And women have now found that out. It all has to do with women, or the homemaker, leaving the home and realizing that where they've gone is not as fabulous, or as rewarding, or as self-fulfilling as the balance between the workplace and the home place.

Having Siblings Has Everything to Do with Why I Don't Like to Share

I have two siblings, and I like sharing my space with my husband, but I don't want to share my space with another woman. Ever. I hated having roommates. I'll give you anything, but when I lend something I have to let go of it, otherwise I'll get all weird about it. I'd rather just give it to you for good and move on, because I have a weird attachment to things, which I know isn't appropriate. It's stupid—but I'd rather just cut my ties to the thing you're borrowing than lend it and have to wonder if it's ever coming back or if it's going to be destroyed. Or stretched. It makes me nervous, which is silly.

And the rifling thing I can't stand, even though, in theory, I have nothing to hide. I want to hide everything—not from the people who live in my house, but from someone else. I don't want anyone in my stuff. It's that "Get off my lawn" mentality, and it's because I had siblings and I never felt like I had privacy.

—JENNIFER

We're cutting in again here to flag another rare appearance of some good stories. If you don't like the good stories, just skim this part. Don't worry: more bad stories are coming.

True Confession: I'm Close to My Family

I speak to my sister five to ten times a day. I speak to my brother every few days and e-mail him every day. I speak to my father at least once a day, and I'm in touch with my husband all day long. When I was young, my grandparents lived with us until they died. My mother always told me I'd end up being best friends with my sister when I grew up, which I found very annoying at the time, but that's exactly how it worked out. None of us have ever been estranged. Our fights don't last more than a few minutes, and we're into forgiveness. Our family is a

You're Not the Only One Whose Parents Had *Lolita* and *The Joy of Sex* in Their Drawer

Alexis: Do your kids know where babies come from?

Jennifer: Yes. We believe in being open and teaching our kids about sex.

Alexis: How did you do it?

Jennifer: I think they asked early on. First of all, they have older cousins, so they'd heard things before we got a chance to tell them. Not to mention TV and movies. It's hard to avoid the subject, so they should know what it is.

Alexis: So they're ready.

Jennifer: Not so they're ready! I think all kids should be educated, because they're going to hear things on the playground, they're going to get misinformation, but with my kids, we'll laugh about stuff. My rule is you have to ask me questions about what you saw. You need to tell me what you don't understand. How did you learn about sex?

Alexis: I don't know. I read a lot when I was a kid.

Jennifer: Dirty books?

Alexis: My parents had a copy of *Lolita* in their drawer—because I went through every drawer. And *The Joy of Sex* had just come out, and they had it. Everybody had it. It was such a big deal. I looked at every picture.

Jennifer: Of course you did.

Alexis: So just leave that lying around in your kids' room, and they'll learn all they need to know.

typical tight-knit Jewish family. It's like we know we're stuck with each other, so we might as well get along.

My siblings used to torture me when I was little because I was the baby, but they let me sleep in their rooms when I got scared. In the middle of the night, I'd grab two pillows and a blanket from the hall closet and sleep on the other bed in my brother's room.

My mother, Bunny, was a piece of work. She was wacky, hilarious, gorgeous, and loving. When I was growing up, my house was the place everybody came to hang out. She wanted it that way. Twenty-four hours a day, kids would come in and out and the phone would ring, and my mother didn't care: she didn't work outside the home, and her kids were her life, so she wanted us around. When my friends came over, they'd go into my parents' room and they'd sit on the bed with my mother, because she was warm and generous and told it like it was. She'd get right in there with the girls, and they loved that.

In October 2007 she was diagnosed with pancreatic cancer. When she was dying and could barely speak, four friends of mine, my sister, and I were all in the hospital room hanging out and talking about something really lame: what someone had had for dinner the night before. And my mother put up her hand and mouthed, Boring! She wanted to dish. She wanted to dish about something salacious or interesting or obnoxious. She wasn't satisfied with the conversation, and even though she could barely talk and was only kind of with it she made sure we knew it.

—JENNIFER

To Alexis, there's nothing creepier and scarier than a happy family. That's why she's going to do things differently with her kids.

Happy Families Freak Me Out

I think people who are *superclose* to their families are completely bizarre. I mean, look at Jennifer and her sister. They still live at home, basically, next door to each other, in houses built on the same piece of property they grew up on. That extreme family closeness thing makes no sense to me. I just don't like when people pretend to be happy all the time and pretend that everyone in their family gets along, then try to make me feel like an asshole for being "grumpy."

Not that Jennifer does this, but there are other people who do. Being dishonest like that might be the socially acceptable behavior, but it's an abhorrent thing to me. Just because I'm not faking it makes me a sucky person? Screw you. There are all kinds of different ways to deal with problematic families. I choose to be honest about it and not pretend. I try not to burden people with my family issues—it's not my goal to put my personal crap out there—but I don't know why I should lie about it all the time, either. Just because I'm related to you doesn't mean we have anything in common, or anything to talk about, and it certainly doesn't mean I can't see through your bullshit.

Now that I have a child any decision I make will take into account how it will affect her. I'll consider things in a much deeper way than my parents did. There's not going to be moving without really thinking about whether it's going to be better for my children or whether it could destroy them—I wouldn't

Oops!

I once took disappearing ink and sprayed it all over my mother's antique sheets. She stripped the bed and washed them and wouldn't talk to me for two days. She was furious even though the ink *disappeared* in the wash.

—ALEXIS

do that to them. Maybe I'll end up making a decision they don't like or that might be difficult for them, but it'll be a seriously thought-out decision.

I'd expose them to much more than I was exposed to. Normal stuff like ice-skating. I didn't even know how to throw a ball or a Frisbee until about five years ago, when I had to ask a friend to teach me. I could play field hockey, clove an orange, and create a recipe, but I couldn't throw a ball. How sad is that? You need to learn things like that so you can get along with other kids and have fun. Sure, reading is fundamental, but there are other things in life.

My parents started their divorce bullshit when I was around twenty, but it took forever. They should have gotten divorced a long time before that. I went to boarding school in ninth grade—I wanted to go. I wanted to be out of the house—being around two people who were so unhappy with each other was debilitating, and their misery was inevitably thrown my way. I went to the wrong boarding school at first—it was a really preppy clean school, which turned out to be exactly like the school and town I'd just left, so then I went to a hippie boarding school with no television, where you could actually be an individual and not have to conform. I was regimented enough—I didn't need someone else to regiment me!

—ALEXIS

I Grew Up with More Pets Than People

We had tons of animals: Chickens. Geese. Lots of birds. Turkeys. Goats. Sheep. Dogs. Cats. We had a keeshond and then chows, and then when I got my own dogs, I got bulldogs. I was trapped by them, a slave to my dogs for twelve years. I did anything for them. I fed them by hand. If I didn't hear the dogs snoring, I'd get up and go downstairs to make sure they were still breathing. People say that's what happens when you have kids (and it does!), but it didn't happen to my mother.

—ALEXIS

Fear Factor

When I was young, I was afraid of bees. Really afraid. And I'd never been stung. So my mother took me to the "Bee Guy" and we bought a queen and all the other bees, put them in the back of the Suburban, and set up the hive. Whenever I hated something, like bees or cooked onions, she'd incorporate that fear or hatred into virtually everything. With the bees, she'd torture me and say, "Oh, we got bees! Isn't it wonderful?" My mother's been stung tons of times, but she always wore all the protective gear and didn't care. My father was allergic, and I used to hide the Epi-Pen.

And for the record, having a hive at the house did *not* make me any less afraid.

—ALEXIS

Neither of us loves the Christmas holidays.

You're Not the Only One Who Hated Christmas

There's not a Christmas I want to remember. Okay, the truth is there was *one*, when I was four or five. Aside from that, it was not a great time. It's not Christmas unless you're swearing and trying to untangle a huge mess of lights, so believe me, too much effort was made to make everything look perfect. But that's just me. I don't think there needs to be a Christmas tree in every room—*every room*. We also had to make gingerbread houses when I was growing up. Huge gingerbread houses. And the gingerbread houses were not kid-friendly. Martha was not interested in being kid-friendly. And these houses were definitely not kid-friendly. Thankfully, I got to stop decorating at an early age because I went away to boarding school.

My mother used to have me wrap my own presents. She would hand me things right before Christmas and say, "Now wrap these, but don't look inside." So I didn't. Because I knew it was never worth looking.

—ALEXIS

Martha Remembers Christmas (a Little Differently Than Alexis Does)

A fresh blanket of snow had fallen and it was hard to walk. Little Bear, our silver keeshond, struggled, and Alexis kept falling and laughing, the snow, in places, deeper than she was tall. We found a perfect tree, a fir covered with its own small pinecones, and sawed it down and dragged it back to the cottage. We stood it in our living room and decorated it with homemade ornaments—cookies, paper chains, strings of cranberries, popcorn, and pinecones, and origami creations that Alexis and I made from colorful papers Andy had brought from Japan.

While we worked, we listened to National Public Radio from Amherst on our old console radio. They played music by Bach and Handel and readings from great writers like Dickens, O. Henry, and Hans Christian Andersen. We laughed and talked and finished the tree, thinking it was the most beautiful thing we had ever seen. It smelled so good and fresh.

Alexis was a very thoughtful child, and buying gifts for her was not difficult. I searched the bookstores for books that I had loved as a child, or ones that seemed perfect to me for that time. I read aloud to her a lot, so some of the books were ones that could be read aloud and understood then, and saved for perusal later on when she could handle all the words herself. We opened our presents on Christmas Eve, after we had eaten a country dinner cooked entirely on the wood-burning range. We had roast duck, sweet potatoes, and apple tart. The pastry, the skin of the duck, the caramelized flesh of the potatoes—I remember it as if it were yesterday.

I'm a Jew Who Thinks Jews Who Have Christmas Trees Are Really Weird

Jews don't work in gingerbread. It's not our medium. And to me, Jews who have trees are weird. And there's no such thing as a Hanukkah bush. If you're Jewish, don't have a Christmas tree. They're beautiful. I love the smell. I love seeing them in other people's houses. Just for that day it would be fun to have one. But it's not our holiday. You don't have a Christmas tree if you're a Jew!

—JENNIFER

Jenny celebrating Christmas with Barbra Streisand.

How Alexis and Jennifer Survive the Christmas Holidays

Alexis

Schedule a trip far away far in advance so you have to "miss" the holidays.
Drink.
Have a blowout (tire, not hair) on the way there and never show up.
Just say no.

Jennifer

Prayer
Positive thinking
Xanax

Make no mistake: Jennifer's childhood wasn't all good. Here comes the Koppelman version of craziness, which involved bodyguards, a private police patrol, and lots and lots of limousines.

Police Patrolled Our Driveway

I don't remember when the bodyguard thing started—I think when I came home from college there was one in the house— but I do remember an awkward booty call with a friend of mine, and the bodyguard had to let him in at two in the morning. We had a bodyguard for the same reason my parents wouldn't let us go anywhere without a limousine: they were afraid we'd be kidnapped. We also had the police patrol our driveway—they still do, actually—but when I was little I could look out my window and see them parked there, so I wouldn't be afraid. Obviously my fears were indulged.

I was raised to fear everything. I try not to focus on my fears. I'm not over them, but I'm much better than I was. I've forced myself to do things because I knew if I didn't, I'd end up crippled and paralyzed by fear. My kids know that I struggle with an irrational level of anxiety, and my goal is for them not to be like me. I want them to find a balance between being careful and being independent. I grew up thinking that if I took the train or drove somewhere by myself, I'd get captured or kidnapped. My sister is doing a great job with her daughter: my niece not only takes the train everywhere but travels all around New York City by herself.

I'm sure it's because my mother isn't alive to say, "Are you nuts?" But it's a great example for me, because now I know that when a kid is fifteen or sixteen, she can take the Long Island Railroad and go to Manhattan and run around the city, and she can get to where she's going and learn how to be independent and street-smart. As long as you know your risks—what they are and where they are—you can do anything. You have to figure out a way to balance how you were raised and how you are raising your kids.

I didn't have a curfew because I had a driver, but when I was at the age that I was driving myself, I always had to drive with friends at night. I wasn't allowed to drive alone at night until I was, like, thirty. It's absurd! So my friends had to follow me home from where we were in separate cars—which is ridiculous, since once my friends made sure I got home safely, no one made sure *they* got home safely.

—JENNIFER

My Mother Called Me an Asshole When I Told Her I Was Moving Out at the Age of Twenty-Three

When I was twenty-three and told my mother that I was moving out of the house and into Manhattan, she called me an asshole. I had gone off to college, but I had come home all the time, and I lived at home during my first year of law school, so she couldn't understand how I could possibly want to move out for good. She thought that was the strangest, most ridiculous thing. My father was supportive of my wanting to live on my own—he wanted me to do things, like work. My sister never moved out—she went to college and then moved back home. My brother had moved out, but he was a boy. Big difference.

My mother ultimately got over it. Her fear that something would happen to me was definitely at the root of her anger: she was so afraid that she had to get mad at me. A lot also had to do with what being a stay-at-home mother (possibly) did to my mom. I'm sure she would have had a much more fulfilling life had she felt validated in other ways, outside her family. When your whole existence is just about taking care of others, whether it's your kids or your spouse or people in general, then you can be left with no identity other than that. And that, to me, is brutal. It also puts a really big responsibility on the children—my kids should know that they're the most important thing to me, and they are—but they should also know that they can grow and flourish and live (even outside the house) and I'll be just fine.

—JENNIFER

Now for a quick change of pace.

Alexis's Childhood Montage

I walked in on my parents having sex. I didn't really see anything, but my mother yelled at me for not knocking. No one ever knocked in our house, and they had a lock on the door that they could have used.

We never had a paper plate in the house. Maybe at a picnic, but never at the house. When I was growing up, being at the table was really casual—my mother wasn't a stickler for place settings and all that crap back then, and by the time she got crazy about it I'd already left the house for boarding school. The annoying thing now is that she loves using rough linen dishcloths as napkins to discourage you from actually using them. She calls them "lapkins."

I used to clean out my mother's closet—the whole closet was half the size of a coffee table. She didn't ask me to do it; I just did it because I couldn't stand how messy it was. Halfway through I'd get overcome with fatigue and depression, but I had to finish. It would take an entire day.

Most of my clothes were in a dresser drawer that was in the hallway, and after I had straightened my stuff I'd go downstairs and say, "Hey! I cleaned out my dresser!" And my mother would say, "If you hadn't made it messy in the first place, you wouldn't need to clean it out."

There were unspoken rules in my house. I didn't really do anything wrong except have a "bad attitude." The fear of getting yelled at was enough to keep me from doing anything wrong, although I'm not sure I would have had that inclination anyway. My mother used to tell me not to come home. She would practically hand me the vodka bottle and a $100 bill and say, "Go buy some drugs and don't come back." I'm exaggerating, of

Alexis feeding the pet rabbits.

course, but I remember her just wanting me to "be social." I've never been a social butterfly, which, for some reason, she thinks she would have wanted or preferred me to be.

Everybody's parents tell them they can be whatever they want to be, but they too often leave out: not unless you really want to, and it's not going to be fun, and here's what you have to do to get there. Nobody ever says anything like that. Or mentions passion and talent. Or admits that it's not just going to come your way by itself—and it might not come your way even if you do everything right. I was led to believe that because I did all my homework and was responsible that that was good enough. And it wasn't good enough.

—ALEXIS

I'm Probably the Only One Who Hobnobbed with (This Partial List of) Famous Musicians because My Father Was a Major Player in the Music Industry When I Was Growing Up

The Lovin' Spoonful
Bobby Darin
Janis Ian
Glen Campbell
Dolly Parton
Paul Anka
Cher
Eddie Murphy
The Four Tops
Barbra Streisand
Tracy Chapman
Vanilla Ice
Wilson Phillips
Arrested Development
Jon Secada

I Could've Been a Contender! (Maybe)

I knew Dolly Parton when I was growing up—she was super-sweet to me—and when I was eight, she said that my sister would be a homemaker (she is), my brother would be an entertainer (he's a successful screenwriter and producer), and I would be a star. Before you vomit, these were *her* words! And no, not there yet. She thought I had a great voice, but because my father was in the music business and knew so much about it, he didn't encourage me to pursue it as a career. Back then, if you wanted to sing, you had to be a songwriter, too. There weren't people like Britney Spears who performed but didn't write songs—there was Barbra Streisand, Lionel Richie, Dolly, and others who did both. My father also knew that I wasn't going to be a pop star—I was too sensitive, I wasn't confident enough, and I didn't have that kind of drive and fight in me. Years later, I realized he was right. My daughter is really talented, and I think she has real potential and is much more suited for it than I was.

—JENNIFER

Aнd last, but certainly not least, the cornerstone of any person's
family and childhood and the heart of this chapter: mothers.

You're Not the Only One Who's Convinced Your Mother Doesn't Like You

My mother hates my personality. And she'll really hate me writing this. Well, where do you want me to go from here? She's
always telling me to "Stop doing the shtick." And I say, "This is
not a shtick. It's just who I am." And so when I go on the radio,
I'm just being who I am. She doesn't know how to react,
because other people laugh and like the show, and she doesn't
know what to do with that.

—ALEXIS

Mom Phone Call Mad-Lib

I used to talk to my mother all the time, and our conversations
went something like this:

> Jennifer: Mom, I'm having an issue with _____
> and I feel like I need some help dealing with it.

> Bunny: What you really need to deal with is _____ ,
> not _____ .

> Jennifer: Mom, why do you have to bring up _____
> when I wanted help with _____? Can't you just
> help me with what I feel I need help with?

Martha on Alexis Redux

Alexis is not always grumpy.
She was always discriminating.
But she wants to be perceived
as grumpy. The no smiling
started, I think, in college. I
always took pictures of her,
tried to make her smile for my
photographs, and my photographs of her are beautiful. All
I care about is that she's happy
and healthy and leads the life
she wants to lead. She's her
own person. She makes up her
own mind. I sometimes try
to offer advice, but if it's not
taken, so be it. She really did
pay attention. She really does
know how to do everything.
And still chooses not to follow
in my footsteps.

Bunny: Jenny, why can't I comment about _____?

Jennifer: Because I wasn't asking about _____, I was asking about _____.

—JENNIFER

Welcome Home! Your Dog Died

I didn't grow up with a lot of pets, but I always had a dog. I had a standard poodle, and then we got a Great Dane. My poodle died when we were away on vacation. We came home, I walked in the house, and the housekeeper was there, and I said, "Where's Sugar?" And her response was, "Oh, she died." It was awful.

—JENNIFER

Why I Call My Mother Martha Instead of Mom

I'm not really sure when I started calling my mother Martha, but it's not some kind of big Freudian thing. I think there just came a time when yelling "Mom!" in public seemed odd to me and inefficient—there is undoubtedly more than one mom in the crowd.

—ALEXIS

Where Am I Going This Weekend? Prison!

I visited Martha a lot when she was unfairly imprisoned. I mean, if shlepping to West Virginia almost every weekend for five months isn't love, then I don't know what is. But seriously, it's what any daughter would have done under the circumstances. There wasn't a question in my mind about visiting her when she wanted me to. Was it a bit annoying when I showed up and there were three other people already entertaining her? Sure! But she needed to know, tangibly, that she wasn't alone, and that was an easy thing for me to do for her.

—ALEXIS

Say *Everything* When a Parent Is Dying

My advice to people who have a dying parent is to get it all out. Get it all out! Even if—and *especially* if—your relationship with that parent is complicated. And most parent-child relationships *are* complicated. Your gripes, concerns, disappointments, successes—everything that made you angry, that made you happy—you need to tell your dying parents all of it. Ask all of the questions you have, tell them you love them and how they made you amazing and also a little insane and a lot angry. Laugh about it. Cry about it. Just talk. Because until someone is gone, we can work through everything and heal so much. When you know that someone has a terminal illness, there doesn't have to be anything left unsaid.

I was lucky, even with an overbearing and somewhat crazy mom, that I never felt unloved or unappreciated. Yes, I felt too fat, and my mom definitely placed more importance on my appearance than was necessary, but ultimately I knew I was her sunshine. While she was sick we had plenty of conversations—about the good, the bad, the ugly—and I am so soothed now, almost three years later, that I told her everything I needed to tell her.

Two days before my mother died, after telling me that she loved me, she said, "I'm sorry." And although I don't know what she was referring to exactly, I believe she meant she was sorry for all of it: for mothering me too much in some ways and too little in other ways; for getting sick; for dying; for leaving me before I could ever be ready for her to go. That last conversation of ours was a gift I'll never stop being grateful for, even on the days when I still can't believe how sad and unfair it is that a woman as beautiful and as young as my mother is gone.

—JENNIFER

7

What Do You Mean You "Can't" Cook?

Alexis and Jennifer on Cooking and Kitchenphobia

෴

Mageirocophobia, or fear of cooking, is extremely common, although it is only considered a phobia when it is severe enough to interfere with daily life. Most people with a fear of cooking fear one or more elements or possible outcomes of the cooking process including: Fear of Causing Illness; Fear of Serving Inedible Food; Presentation Concerns; Fear of the Cooking Process; and Fear of Recipes.

Adapted from About.com

There is no one who *can't* cook—only people who *won't* cook. The first thing you have to do in order to get over whatever it is you don't like about cooking is figure out what's behind it. Not to get all Freudian on you, but most aversions are caused by your parents. Freud would say that the reason Alexis is so obsessed with the kitchen is that she's trying to one-up her mother. And he'd say that Jennifer stopped cooking for a while because she cooked a lot for her mother before she died.

Everyone should have a couple of go-to recipes for when they need them. Not everyone has to love cooking, because not everybody does. If you do, that's great, but even if you don't, you should learn how to make certain basic things. It's easy to make pasta. And if you're not a vegetarian, you should know how to roast a chicken.

Anyone can make anything. All you do is follow a recipe. You can make a soufflé and impress everybody, and it takes ten minutes. Throw some salad in a bowl, make some vinaigrette with oil and vinegar, salt and pepper. Now you've impressed the pants off everybody, and it tastes good. Keep reading for a whole list of Alexis and Jennifer's most impressive dishes made with minimal skill and effort.

Why I Started Cooking

I started cooking and baking and making my own food when I was young because I had to. Once my mother became a caterer, she forgot to feed her own family. I'd say, "I'm hungry!" and she'd respond, "That's okay!"

—ALEXIS

You're Probably the Only One Who Went to "Cooking School"

When I was little, my friends and I had to go to "cooking school" at my house. It was after regular school. And we had to wear those stupid little chef's hats. They're called toques. I think Martha did it because she thought it would be fun. People like to think that Martha didn't pay attention to me, but it's just not true. Maybe it wasn't the right kind of attention, but it was attention all right.

—ALEXIS

Talking to Larry King

Larry King: What was it like to grow up with a mom that's a perfectionist?

Alexis Stewart: She was my mom, and as everyone knows, I'm a better cook and more of a perfectionist than my mother.

King: Good. Get your own show. Do something.

Jenny and Alexis filming *Whatever, Martha!*

Being an Obsessive Baker and an Obsessive Cleaner Is a Problem

I guess you could call me a compulsive baker. Anyone who reads my blog knows that I go on baking sprees and cook in bulk often. But baking and cooking that much makes everything dirty, which bothers me, so my compulsions clash—the cleaning and the cooking.

—ALEXIS

Alexis's pots and pans.

I Bake Incessantly, but I Rarely Eat or Taste What I Bake

The fact that I bake a lot and hardly ever eat what I bake makes a lot of people angry. They think I have an eating disorder, which is ridiculous. I bake because it's a creative outlet for me. And my real poison is crunchy and salty—or cheesy! So the cookies can sit there, but hide the red wine, French bread, and cheese.

I bake when I am dating and when I am single. I baked when I was married, and I bake now that I'm divorced. I bake whenever I fucking feel like it. Sometimes Martha uses my ideas and recipes on her show or in her magazine, so I guess you could say it's work-related, too. As for why I don't taste what I bake: the best way to not eat any is to not taste it. I'm of the opinion that baked goods rarely need to be tasted until it's too late to fix them, anyway (that is, when they come out of the oven). If you never let the batter or icing touch your lips, you won't feel the need to eat any, but once you start tasting, all bets are off!

—ALEXIS

You're Not the Only One Who Feels Bad When You Cook for Other People and They Don't Give You a Big Enough Reaction

Jennifer: Do you like cooking for other people?

Alexis: When I cook for people, I ask them if they like it, and if they do, I'm very happy.

Jennifer: What if they don't say anything?

Alexis: I feel bad, but I don't get angry.

Jennifer: You don't? If you don't get a big enough reaction to what you've made, you get all freaked out!

Alexis: Well, I feel bad, but it doesn't mean I'm mad at them. It means I wish they'd enjoyed it a little more. *And* kissed my ass a little more.

You're Probably the Only One Who Invented a Cookie Recipe for Martha Stewart When You Were Thirteen

I invented a recipe for chocolate chip cookies when I was a kid. My mother was catering, and one of the cooks who worked for her made these amazing cookies, and my mother wanted the recipe. So she gave my mother the recipe, but then the next day she came crying to her and said that she hadn't given her the real recipe because she just couldn't give it to her. I was thirteen or fourteen at the time, and it took me two tries to figure it out. At first Martha called them Alexis's Famous Chocolate Chip Cookies, but then she changed it to Alexis's Brown Sugar Chocolate Chip Cookies. Both names are annoying.

—ALEXIS

Oh, Alexis, Why the Cookie Shame?

Jennifer: You should be proud of yourself.

Alexis: For making up a cookie recipe when I was thirteen?

Jennifer: You know, you're such a loser because you can't embrace that you have a talent for cooking and baking. It doesn't mean it's the only thing that defines you. I think the fact that you're a whore defines you!

Alexis: Thank you! That's infinitely preferable and flattering to me. And whore is not the correct word—slut, maybe, but not whore.

"These cookies went to my endocrinologist to try to bribe him to be extra nice to me."—Alexis

~

**Martha Whittles Her Own Reusable Birchwood
S'mores Sticks**

Alexis: I never liked s'mores. I only ate them because I thought I was supposed to like them. Martha's s'mores are totally over the top. That's because she makes her own birch-twig marshmallow-roasting sticks. She has an endless supply of birch twigs.

Jennifer: That's ridiculous! You grab a stick off a tree, you shove a marshmallow on it—boom!—and then you put it over the campfire. That's it!

Alexis: Maybe for a normal person. But Martha *whittles* her own birch twig. And then she sandpapers the end of it. Why? So the marshmallow doesn't get a splinter? Then she drills a hole in the stick so you can hang it up.

Jennifer: But marshmallow twigs don't get reused.

Alexis: Apparently they do! She makes them so they can be used forever.

Jennifer But they get covered in melted marshmallow goo.

Alexis: I guess you sandpaper the goo off the stick every time you're done with it.

Jennifer Are you kidding me?

Alexis: No. And yes. And then she uses wax-covered linen string to hang them up. Where—in the s'mores closet? Then she bundles the sticks! As if it wasn't enough that she made them. Now they have to be bundled?

My Parents Bought Only Rum Raisin Ice Cream

My parents would occasionally go out and buy a pint of Häagen-Dazs ice cream. And guess what flavor it would be? Rum raisin. Always. They had a child—me—and that's what they'd buy? I mean, sometimes I would eat it out of desperation, but I hated every bite because it was (and is) disgusting.

—ALEXIS

I Make My Own Red Wine Vinegar

Every time I have a glass of red wine and I don't finish it, I put it in an open-mouthed jar with some organic unpasteurized cider vinegar mother/starter from the health-food store. And every time I don't finish a bottle, I dump it in there, too, and now I have fabulous fancy red wine vinegar!

—ALEXIS

Some of Alexis's cookbooks.

Chicken on a Caesar Salad—Wrong!

It's depressing when you go to a restaurant and they ask you if you want grilled chicken or shrimp on your Caesar salad. That's when you know it's going to be a bad salad.

—ALEXIS

A Caesar without Anchovies

I like Caesar salad without anchovies—not even in the dressing. Is that still a Caesar salad?

—JENNIFER

No.

—ALEXIS

For Those of You Taking Notes at Home: Clinical Terms for Food-Related Fears

Fear of peanut butter sticking to roof of mouth	arachibutyrophobia
Fear of meat	carnophobia
Fear of food	sitophobia
Fear of vegetables	lachanophobia

Alexis and Jennifer's Most Impressive Dishes Made with Minimal Skill and Effort

All you really need to know to get around in the kitchen is how to make these basic dishes and beverages, so easy they could be completed by a kindergartner. Making these will teach you basic techniques without your even being aware of how much you're learning. Then you can tweak them into hundreds of iterations, and no one will realize how often they're eating the same thing over and over.

The Basics

- Coffee
- Toast
- Scrambled eggs
- Broiled chicken parts
- Mashed potatoes
- Gravy
- Pasta with garlic and oil
- Salad with vinaigrette
- Haricots verts or string beans
- Pie with homemade crust or a "crumble"
- Noodle pudding

Make each of these recipes just once, and we promise you'll never not want to cook again.

Alexis's Recipes

When you cook or bake, the ingredients you use must be of the highest quality. The best ingredients will make a huge difference in the taste of the food. Always use the freshest vegetables and fruits and the highest-quality dairy and eggs (preferably local), and use organic everything as often as possible. Even the quality of your flour matters.

Perfect Chocolate Chip Cookies

MAKES 50 4-INCH COOKIES

1 pound (4 sticks) unsalted butter, room temperature, plus more for greasing baking sheets

3 cups packed light-brown sugar

1 cup granulated sugar

4 large eggs

2 teaspoons pure vanilla extract

3½ cups all-purpose flour

1½ teaspoons salt

2 teaspoons baking soda

1½ cups best-quality chocolate chips

This recipe produces flat and crispy chocolate chip cookies. Use an ice cream scoop to ensure a uniform size and even baking. If the cookies harden before you have a chance to remove them from the baking sheet, return the sheet to the oven for a few seconds to soften the dough for easier removal.

Preheat oven to 375 degrees Fahrenheit. Grease or line two baking sheets with Silpat baking mats or parchment; set aside. In a large bowl, cream butter until smooth; add sugars and beat until smooth. Beat in eggs and vanilla. In another large bowl, sift together flour, salt, and baking soda. Slowly beat dry ingredients into wet mixture. Fold in chocolate chips.

Drop 2 or 3 tablespoons dough per cookie onto greased or parchment-covered baking sheets; space dough at least 2 inches apart to allow for spreading. Bake until golden, 8 to 10 minutes. Remove cookies from baking sheets and allow to cool on baking racks.

Note: this recipe can be tricky; you may need to bake just one or two cookies to see if the batter needs more flour if the cookies are too thin.

Scrambled Eggs

SERVES 2

Get thee to a farmer's market, if possible. Why? Because the best eggs make the best scrambled eggs, and it's just the right thing to do, for you and for the environment. As for toast to serve with these eggs, I keep sliced bread from Balthazar Bakery, Poilane, or Pain Quotidien in the freezer so I always have great bread for toasting at the ready. I know it's none of my business what kind of toaster you use, but I love my Breville Toaster Oven.

butter or olive oil to taste

3-4 large fresh cage-free eggs

salt and freshly ground pepper to taste

good bread for toasting

Heat a heavy pan over medium heat with more butter than you think you'll need (if you're just cooking for yourself, use less, or just a touch of olive oil).

Crack eggs into bowl. Whisk until slightly fluffy.

When pan is ready, pour in eggs. As they solidify, gently stir or scramble with a wooden spoon or a spatula. Remove pan from heat when eggs are almost cooked through but still wet, and continue to stir until almost cooked. Do not overcook.

Serve on a prewarmed plate with plenty of salt and pepper and buttered toast.

Shallot Vinaigrette

SERVES 2

1 shallot, minced

½ cup *fino* sherry or, in a pinch, sherry vinegar

1 tablespoon Dijon mustard

1 tablespoon honey

⅓ cup sherry vinegar

⅓ cup olive oil

⅓ cup grapeseed oil

salt and pepper to taste

One of the problems with some Americans is that they use bottled salad dressing. Why do they do this? Because for some reason they think making fresh salad dressing is hard. It's not hard; it's easy. It takes only a few minutes and a few ingredients, and it's a lot healthier and better tasting than the bottled crap you're used to.

Combine minced shallot and sherry or vinegar in a small saucepan. Boil until almost all the sherry or vinegar has evaporated.

Combine cooled shallot-infused vinegar and cooked shallots with Dijon mustard, honey, additional sherry vinegar, olive oil, grapeseed oil, salt, and pepper. Transfer mixture to a jar, shake well, and pour over leafy greens (such as Bibb lettuce) or vegetables just before serving.

Haricots Verts or String Beans

fresh *haricots verts* or string beans (one handful for each person)

lemon juice, freshly squeezed

No, they're not the same thing. Haricots verts is French for "green bean," but haricots verts are longer and thinner and more tender than American green beans. Also, they taste better. And not just because they're French.

Steam or boil beans in a large pot until crunchy but tender. Drain and serve immediately, sprinkled with lemon juice or shallot vinaigrette.

Roast Chicken

SERVES 2 TO 4

Find the best chicken parts you can from a local farm or a farm that raises its poultry in a sustainable and humane manner (check out http://www.farmforward.com). Otherwise, you'll be eating chickens that lived in extreme confinement: huge, dark, overcrowded sheds reeking of feces, ammonia and filth, and air thick with feathers. Sorry, but it's true. Organic chicken can now be found in most supermarkets, and even though it's a little more expensive than crappy chicken, it's worth it. At least, to me it is. You might not mind eating gross food, but I refuse to.

fresh organic chicken parts

half-sweet paprika

salt and pepper

Preheat oven broiler.

Place chicken parts on a foil-lined baking pan. Sprinkle with paprika, salt, and pepper.

Broil for approximately 10 minutes per side—turn, cook for another 10 minutes, then turn them once more, skin side up, until pieces are fully cooked.

Perfect served hot, cold, or at room temperature.

Beurre Rouge (Red Wine Butter Sauce)

SERVES 4

1 bottle good red wine

1 shallot, finely chopped

½ stick butter, cubed

salt

Pour wine into a shallow pot and add shallot. Heat until reduced to about ⅓–½ cup liquid.

Add butter. Whisk until smooth. Add salt to taste. Strain if desired.

Serve immediately over steak (grass-fed beef and served only rare), chicken, or other meats.

Berry Crisp or Crumble

This is the easiest dessert ever. You can make a double, triple, or quadruple batch of topping mixture and freeze it to make this dessert anytime.

SERVES 8

Preheat oven to 375 degrees Fahrenheit.

In a medium bowl, combine berries or other fruit with sugar, flour, and lemon juice. Set aside.

In another bowl, add flour, brown sugar, rolled oats, cinnamon, salt, and butter. Combine with your fingers until all the butter is evenly distributed and in small clumps. Sprinkle over berries or fruit (or a combination) and bake in a lightly greased Pyrex or ceramic baking dish or pie plate for about an hour or until the fruit is bubbling and the topping is browned.

Berry or fruit mixture

6-8 cups fresh or frozen berries (or 8-10 peaches, sliced—they can be frozen, too—if using frozen do not thaw before baking)

¼-⅓ cup sugar

⅓ cup flour

juice of ½ lemon

Topping

1 cup all-purpose flour

¾ cup brown sugar

1 cup rolled oats

pinch of cinnamon

pinch of salt

9 tablespoons butter, unsalted, room temperature

Bunny Koppelman's Noodle Pudding

SERVES 6 TO 8

2 packages (24 ounces) egg noodles

2 packages (16 ounces) cream cheese

2⅔ cups sugar

6 eggs, separated

2 teaspoons vanilla extract

2 cups apricot nectar

1 cup milk

2 sticks butter plus extra to butter pan

3 cups cornflake crumbs

Preheat oven to 350 degrees Fahrenheit.

In a large pot, cook the noodles in salted water, then drain and add one stick of butter to the hot noodles.

While the noodles are cooking, in a medium bowl mix the cream cheese with 2 cups of the sugar until the mixture is smooth. Add the egg yolks, vanilla, apricot nectar, and milk.

In a separate bowl, beat the 6 egg whites, then fold into the cream cheese mixture.

Add the slightly cooled buttered noodles to the cream cheese mixture. Pour the mixture into a greased casserole dish.

To make the topping:

Melt one stick of butter in a pan or the microwave and in a small bowl add it to ⅔ cups of sugar and the cornflake crumbs. Sprinkle the cornflake crumb mixture on top of the noodles. Bake for 20 to 30 minutes.

8

Drawing the Line at Fat Elbows

Alexis and Jennifer on Weight Loss and Body Issues

When I was eight, my mother said that if my feet were so ticklish, what was I going to do when a guy wanted to suck on my toes?

Alexis Stewart

∽

I thought men wouldn't like my body because it wasn't perfect, and then they wouldn't like *me*. But guys aren't nearly as discerning as we think they are. They don't really care if you're perfect. They just care if you're naked.

Jennifer Koppelman Hutt

We're not going to sugarcoat this: we're complete opposites when it comes to the topics of weight, body issues, fitness and exercise, and sex. There's not going to be much common ground in our opinions and experiences on these topics; in fact, there may not be *any* common ground. Probably all we agree on is basic cleanliness, good grooming, and Botox. And we're big believers in all three!

It's no secret that Alexis doesn't have a lot of sympathy for fat people, even though she'll deny that—she swears she feels bad for heavy people, especially heavy people who don't exercise. But what really bothers her is the idea that it's not a fat person's fault that he or she is fat. Well, whose fault is it, she wants to know.

Someone once told Alexis that people would kill to have her body. "Sure, they'd kill," she said, "but they won't get up and go for a walk."

Just Move Your Ass

I know why we overeat—because that's what we're programmed to do—but there are people who just don't move. There are people in the office who won't get their own filtered water out of the refrigerator! They're always looking for someone else to get it for them. But all you have to do is walk down the goddamn hallway! It's not like you're *so* involved in your work that you can't get up! You just don't want to move. When I have to do something stupid like clean the floor, I think it's exercise. If I have to walk to the subway, I think, More exercise. That's a great thing about New York: without even thinking about it, you've added two miles to your day. Just give up one thing for a week like soda and drink water instead—and see how much better you feel.

—ALEXIS

Being Fat Is Complicated

Being fat is a very complicated issue for overweight people. Everybody has her own path, and I don't like judging others for how far they've come or not come, because it involves emotions and physiology—and that's all interrelated. I don't think

Jenny at the beach.

it's as simple as willpower. I just don't. And I hate people who do. I hate people who say, "Just go on a diet." Because it's like shedding half of yourself—it's shedding a big part of yourself, and that's got to have a huge impact on you emotionally.

In our society it's very shameful to be fat, which is ironic because so many of us are. Maybe if there was less shame, people would have more success losing weight, because shame breeds anger. When I was fat I felt so angry that I felt shame on a regular basis. And that made me want to say to the world, "Screw you—I'm just going to be fat." But that's really helping no one. It's hurting you. But it makes sense because it comes from this unbelievable frustration and hurt: I'm not good enough because I'm fat? People are very mean to fat people—I know, because at this point I've been on both sides as an adult, and it's screwed up.

—JENNIFER

It's Your Life, and That's *Not* Complicated

I know it's complicated—how you're brought up—but it's your life, and that's *not* complicated. That's the only body you have, and then you're dead. You want to be able to walk around? People seem perfectly content on their little scooters because they're too fat to be able to get up and walk. And I don't think that's a fun life. If you have weight issues and body issues, then get help and make it work for you. Take your health into account and stop whining that you don't have enough money for a personal trainer. Go to the gym or just go for a walk.

Just walk half an hour a day, and it will increase your life expectancy and decrease your chances of getting all these different diseases. I'm not mean to fat people. Sometimes I feel disgusted, sometimes I feel bad, sometimes it pisses me off—I'm pretty angry about the burdens on society that fat people are going to put on us. I know that it's not all their fault. I know there's a difference between smoking cigarettes and overeating—you can live without the cigarette and you can't live without food—but if you can't stop overeating, then get help. Otherwise it's all just another excuse. It might be a valid excuse, but it's still your only body.

So whoever pissed you off wins? Whoever made you fat wins? There are other fun things to do—there are other satisfying things in life. There are. Being the perfect weight? Yeah, that's really tough. It's all tough. You just have to be happy with yourself. Sometimes heavy people can make it work for them. You have a big ass? J Lo has a huge ass. I don't want it. But she's got it and it works for her (obviously she has a lot of other good physical attributes). So try to be healthy and accept what you can't do anything about. You could be really skinny and have a huge ass, and there's nothing you can do about that, either. So fine. Wear clothes that make you look good, and work it!

—ALEXIS

Being Fat and Happy Would Be Easy If People Weren't So Mean

It's hard to be happy with yourself when people are mean to you. I got fat comments when I was on television. Someone called me Jabba the Hutt. That killed me. They might as well have just said, "You're not a person, you're just *fat*." Being perceived as asexual when you're fat and not at all sexy is awful. *Awful.* The presumption that you're not appealing is very sad. Having a voluptuous, curvy ass like J Lo is one thing; being morbidly obese is another thing.

I don't believe in Fat Serenity. I tried Overeaters Anonymous more than ten years ago, and found it totally depressing because there were a lot of women who were very overweight, and they would talk about how they were abstinent and working their programs and how they had serenity even though they were fat. I never had a serene moment when I was fat. And I don't believe in that. I believe in always trying to be the best you, the healthiest you that you can be. Even if you're trying for a very long time. I think you just have to keep trying. You can never throw in the towel; you can never give up and become complacent.

—JENNIFER

Alexis thought she was too fat to fit into her jeans. Whatever!

Nutrition Really Isn't That Hard

I can't stand it when people say they're going to a nutritionist. I say, "You're going to a diet doctor or a diet coach?" Because honestly, nutrition is easy. It might not be fun. It might not be exciting. But it's really easy. It's just not that complicated. Is it more complicated if you're going to ride in the Tour de France? Sure. And even then it's not that complicated. People say they don't know what to eat, but they do. Even my mother pretends she doesn't know what has cholesterol in it. She says she's going on a low-cholesterol diet and then she'll grab a piece of cheese. What?

It's just because you don't want to know. It's just because you don't like the answer. Yeah, the answer isn't fun. I know that. It's not fun. Would I like to only eat bread and cheese? Yes! I'd like to eat it all the time. Cheese, cheese, cheese, cheese, cheese. But I can't. Just because it's not what you want to hear doesn't mean it's not the right answer.

—ALEXIS

Do Whatever It Takes

Here's what I think: whatever you need to do to get healthy, do it. If you feel like you need a diet doctor or a nutritionist, a group, or a trainer, go for it. Spend the money you would have spent on doughnuts and use it to give yourself the help you need to make your body healthy.

—JENNIFER

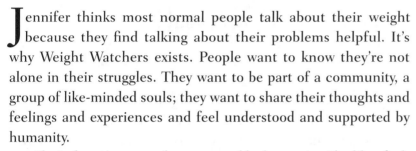

Jennifer thinks most normal people talk about their weight because they find talking about their problems helpful. It's why Weight Watchers exists. People want to know they're not alone in their struggles. They want to be part of a community, a group of like-minded souls; they want to share their thoughts and feelings and experiences and feel understood and supported by humanity.

Alexis doesn't want to be supported by humanity. She likes feeling alone in her struggles—even if she doesn't really have any major body-issue struggles.

Talking about Weight and Dieting Is Incredibly Boring

There's nothing more boring than having to listen to someone talk about her weight or her diet. But it's one of Jennifer's favorite topics. She loves talking about her weight and what she's not eating, and I hate talking about it. I think talking about dieting is one of the most boring things on the planet. You want to lose weight? Here's a news flash for the whole world: eat less, move more, and shut up about it.

I also can't stand when people lose weight and become all about the fact that they've lost weight. I'm like, you've changed, but the world around you is exactly the same. Really, nobody cares but you. I liked you before and I like you now, but if you want me to keep congratulating you every five minutes, that's going to be annoying. It doesn't have anything to do with wanting the person to stay fat. But I don't care. I don't talk about my weight. I don't want to talk about your weight—whether you're fat or thin.

—ALEXIS

This Time I Didn't Talk about It

The last time I lost weight I didn't make a big proclamation, because Alexis always says, "You don't have to announce what you're doing. Just do it and get on with it." So I didn't say anything to anybody, and I just started slowly dieting. Only my husband knew. When people started noticing and asking me about it, I'd just say that I was trying, and then when I kicked it up a notch and started exercising regularly, people started to notice more.

I don't believe in the evangelical approach to weight loss or telling people how to do it—it's different for everyone, and I can't stand people who lose weight and get smug, because there is no smug. It's a day at a time. I never feel like I've got it conquered. Because once you have a weight problem, it's yours forever. It's just how you manage it. Losing weight and getting healthy require selfishness. You have to figure out what you need to get to be where you want to be and not being afraid to say, "This is what works for me, and it doesn't matter what anyone else thinks. This is my truth. This is how I'm gonna do it."

Now I talk about it because people ask. The struggle of being overweight and looking for help is universal. And because

I've been on both sides, I feel enormous compassion for those who struggle, and I'm happy to help. It makes me feel like I'm giving back.

—JENNIFER

Don't Bore Me with Your Eating Issues in a Restaurant

I don't talk about dieting when I'm dieting. And I don't want to hear about anybody else's diet. And I *really* don't want to hear about it in a restaurant. I don't want to hear about it at all. Just do it. Order what you want and don't tell me about it. When I go to a meal with my mother and a bunch of other people, she'll announce that I'm a vegetarian—I'm like Oy, shut up. It's annoying for other people.

No one wants to hear about food issues at the dinner table. It's the same as talking about exercise. No one cares about my workout except me and my trainer. Really. It's not interesting. If you're there to eat a meal, and you don't want to eat, just say, "I'm not hungry" or "I'm on a diet and I hope you don't mind that I'm just going to sit here and not eat anything. I'm going to get a cup of coffee, hope that's okay." Yes it's okay. As long as you don't keep talking about it.

Don't say you're allergic to something if you don't like it— just tell the waiter, "You know what? I hate arugula. Can you please not put it in my food? And if I can't get this without arugula, let me know and I'll get something else." Don't lie to waiters. And be nice. Otherwise they're just going to spit in your food.

I'll often eat one meal a day. It's just the way I am—it works for me. Sometimes I'll eat at four, and sometimes on the weekend I'll just eat dinner. And I'm fine. There might be a moment during the day when I don't feel good, but mostly I'm fine. I have no interest in food anyway until two o'clock, so sometimes I'll have starved myself out of habit and it'll be dinner time.

I'll be meeting someone like my friend Kevin at a panini place that I love because I love crunchy food. But the place doesn't take reservations and it's really small and I'll get there early, but you can't sit down without the other person, so I'll wait outside and I'll almost get hysterical. Because I want my food. But I don't tell anybody about it. I don't tell Kevin about it. I don't tell the waiter about it. Because the waiter doesn't care. He doesn't care that this bitch is really hungry. It's not his problem! Certain things are his responsibility, but the fact that I waited all day to eat is not. So I don't tell anyone—I don't tell anyone that I'm almost crying and all panicked that I haven't had food, because it's *my* fault I didn't have any food.

—ALEXIS

Since Alexis is probably sick of talking about how sick she is of people talking about their weight and dieting, let's change the subject. Let's let Jennifer talk about her weight and dieting.

I Drew the Line at Fat Elbows

My arms never bothered me, and then all of a sudden they did. I guess it was two years ago when I looked at my arms—I look at the back of myself in the mirror when I'm naked in the bathroom at night and getting ready for bed, so every night I can see if my body is smaller and how it's changing. At the time it wasn't getting that much smaller or changing all that much, and one night I noticed that I had fat-lady fat elbows. It's like a glob of fat above the elbow, between the shoulder and elbow.

Like a two-inch blob of fat. Someone only gets that when they're really fat; you're not chubby when you have that— you're *fat* when you have that.

So at that moment I realized I was fat. It was one thing to not want to show my upper arms, but to all of a sudden have my *elbows* be an issue? It was unacceptable. I have good ankles and lovely wrists and forearms, but it didn't matter. *I had fat elbows*. And that was part of the wake-up call. I couldn't handle ever seeing that again. It was horrible. And it helped me to stop shoving food in my mouth.

—JENNIFER

Jennifer's Skinny Jeans

I can't do the "You can never eat this for the rest of your life" kind of thing. That doesn't work for me. I have to give myself permission to eat whatever I want, and by doing that, I'm ultimately able to keep it in check. It's a process. I go through weeks when all I want is peanut butter. So there will be days when I'll have peanut butter and a banana for breakfast, then I'll take a jar of peanut butter with me in my car so I can have some peanut butter for lunch—with a Hershey's Miniature— and then I'll end up eating a little peanut butter for dinner with a yogurt. I mean, it's a joke. And I'll do that for a week. And then I'm over peanut butter and I move on.

There are other days when I have to have salad with grilled chicken. *I have to have that*. And I have to have the *same salad* with the *same grilled chicken* four days in a row. Or I'll go for days where I *have* to eat sushi or when I *can't* eat sushi. I almost never eat pasta—maybe I did once in the past year— but I don't think about it. So my rule is that if I think about it and I really, really want it, then I have to find a way to make it okay to eat it. Weight Watchers is such a good plan because you really can allow any food—but you have to count it. If I really want a Pop-Tart, I'm going to find a way to have it (though I've barely had any in the past couple of years). I eat chocolate all the time. But the chocolate I eat is factored into whatever else I'm having.

I have an unbelievably supportive group of people in my life—my friends are all skinny; I don't have a single fat friend—so they encourage and listen, and we complain about having to watch what we eat and they yell at me and laugh at me. Now when my skinny friends ask me what I want to do for dinner and I say, "I don't know! I don't know what I should eat!" they yell at me and say, "You know, when you were fat you knew what time dinner was, you knew where we were going, who was going, what you were going to eat, and all of a sudden, it's, 'I don't care and I don't know!'" And they're like "Who are you?" All they do is make fun of me—but in a good way.

When I bought my first pair of skinny jeans—my sister and my niece forced me to—I wore them to camp drop-off, and all my friends were talking about how cute I looked in them. They just want to root for me. I don't think I could've accomplished my weight loss without that. We walk together, we take classes together, we train together; it's just nice. There's a study that claims that if you have thin friends, you'll be thinner. So find thin friends. There's truth to that idea in general: if you have healthy relationships, you'll be healthier. If you're in a group of people who encourage one another and support one another, it's much easier to accomplish what you want to accomplish.

My sister doesn't have a weight problem; she's very thin. I mean, she thinks she's fat and she's not—she definitely has body dysmorphic disorder. My mother was oppressive about my body—she made me crazy and definitely added to my fat issues, and who knows if I would've had as much of a weight issue if I'd had a different mother. There was always this push-pull of wanting to do right for myself, but I was so angry with my mother that I hurt myself to spite her, but really I was just spiting myself. It's no surprise that I'm thinner now than I've been since I was twenty-four and my mother's not here. I don't really think that's a coincidence. Mothers have an impact on how we care for ourselves in a big way.

I made a conscious decision to be different with my daughter about food and eating. I was petrified that she'd have a weight problem like I did, and I'm on her constantly because she gets caught up in what kind of body she'll have. My daughter, thankfully, has a healthy appetite, but I require that she move as much as she can so that she does not get fat. I'm not interested in making it like "food doesn't matter, eat whatever you want." I'm a former fatty!

Jenny and her sister, Stacy, during a family vacation

I have a mantra: You have one body, so take care of it. Food is not what you should go to for dealing with boredom. And move, move, move. But none of what I say or do ever makes my daughter feel unloved. She knows I don't equate how she's taking care of her body with how much I do or do not love her. So that's the biggest change. I always felt so judged—I felt hated by my mother if she thought I was fat one week, but that feeling always passed because I knew that she loved me.

My daughter always knows how much I love her, how freaking fantastic I think she is, and that the sun rises and sets on her—and her dad is always making it clear that he feels the same way. She feels like a million bucks, and I'm grateful that my daughter isn't nearly as insecure, the way I was. Then again, she's got an adorable body!

And my son? Well, he doesn't worry about his body. Girls are just different that way.

I'm definitely working through this thinner-me thing— getting to know myself this way. It is way fun to dress inappropriately for my age (not really inappropriate, but my version of that), wearing skinny jeans and trendy tops, shopping and finding clothes in every store, and doing my hair and putting on makeup each day. It's exciting to be looked at for a reason other than being fat. And then I go to a beach for vacation (with a scale I brought from home because yes, I'm crazy), and I'm not being stared at, which is awesome!

I'm blending in. I look like every other normal-sized middle-aged woman, wearing a swimsuit with a short matching skirt, running in and out of the ocean chasing kids or panicking about the waves (okay, so others don't do that). Figuring out what to wear when I was fat was always a tough thing for me, but now I think and dress like a thin person—I'm a size 6 . . . usually! (which is quite thin in the normal world but not in the fashion and entertainment world).

So now, because I can fit into any brand of any clothing, which is really life changing, I think that I can dress like a regular person. I don't stand out for being fat. When I was fat, I didn't want to be seen, but I couldn't avoid being seen. There's no blending in when you're fat. I was never a bright-colored fat dresser. I was always a black-clothes fat dresser. I wear more colors now, and it's so much easier to get dressed, which is such a gift.

—JENNIFER

Back to Alexis's annoyance with the way people think about eating and food. Don't they know that there's more food coming? That it *isn't* cheaper to eat crappy food than healthy food? And that they're not actually going to die if they can't have their coffee—or their bagel, or their muffin, or whatever it is they *have* to have every morning?

There's More Food Coming

People tell themselves or their kids, "You order whatever you want and whatever way you want it." You know what? Grow up. It's one meal. It doesn't have to be exactly the way you want it. Enough with the half-caf-decaf, half soy milk, caramel macchiato. Salad dressing on the side is about as far as I think you should go. No bacon if you don't eat meat, and then shut up. Go home and eat what you want the way you want it, or go out by yourself.

A lot of diet books supposedly say the same thing—I think I've read only one diet book in my whole life—and it's this: there's another meal coming. In this country, for most people, there's more food coming. This isn't the last meal! This isn't the last time you're going to get to eat. So it doesn't have to be what you want, in your heart of hearts. It doesn't have to be your dream meal. It doesn't have to include *everything* you love. You don't have to be *completely* full.

There's more food coming. So relax. Humans are programmed to eat and eat and eat and eat as a way to prepare for not having enough to eat. That's why you have to keep telling yourself that there's more food. So if you can't have it right now—if you deprive yourself of something *this minute*—it doesn't mean you'll never have it. You can have it later. This isn't your last meal.

I don't believe in portion sizes. I eat huge quantities of food. You put a little pasta in front of me, and I'm like "What? You're kidding, right? Because I need five times that amount." It depends on what you've eaten that day. It's all relative. Some people find the size of my lunch horrifying—they look at me and say, "You're going to eat *all* that?" And I say, "Yeah, I'm *really* hungry. Are you going to drink that *entire* Big Gulp?"

I don't want to hear the "It's cheaper" excuse—that it's cheaper to eat badly than to eat healthily—because rice and beans are not fattening; they're very healthy and cheap, and you don't have to make them with lard. You don't have time? Of course you have time. But people aren't willing to give up some of their four-hours-a-day of TV watching to go out of their way to a really good market. I wish we spent a lot more money in this country on education, but even that wouldn't solve the whole problem. I don't think we should feed anybody shit—not in school, not in prison; it doesn't help anything. It doesn't have to be more expensive to feed people food that isn't garbage. Beans without lard are not expensive. It's the cheapest thing on the planet. Rice is cheap.

I'm disgusted by people who can't function without their morning cup of coffee or whatever they eat in the morning or whatever they *have* to have for lunch. Really? Because World War III might be coming, and we're not going to have time to stop and get a cup of coffee. I used to say that to my ex-husband because he couldn't do anything without coffee. I'd say, "So World War III comes, and what, we're going to stop to get you an espresso? Am I going to have to carry you?"

I don't get it. You have to be able to deprive yourself once in a while and survive. What do you mean you can't go without coffee just once? In a way it's cute and in a way it isn't cute. And when people say, "I'm so hungry I'm going to die!" I think, Really? Because you ate breakfast. So go get something.

I don't do stuff with people who I know are going to have to stop and eat—they may be in better shape than I am, with better bodies than mine, but I dread the fact that they'll need to eat, so I'll make them food and bring it along so I don't have to hear about it and so we don't have to go someplace where I'll have to watch them eat something disgusting. I'll just bring food for them with me. Then, inevitably, if I bring the food, they're not hungry!

—ALEXIS

Let's talk about body issues! We know Jennifer's been plagued with them all her life, but the question is: Is there anything Alexis hates about her body—besides her boobs?

Sorry If I (Mostly) Like My Body

I'm not into having breasts, really. They don't keep me up at night—it's not an "issue" per se—I'd just rather not have them. And it's been my experience that nobody touches my boobs. I don't know or particularly care if they're gross, but basically they're ignored. Maybe only ass-men go after me. I don't hate my body or love it. I've just always wanted to have a boy's body.

No boobs. I'd like to be completely flat-chested. I know I'd look weird without breasts, but I'm just not interested in them. I definitely never wanted to have an hourglass figure—I can appreciate it—but I want to be able to move around. That's more important to me.

I started running in sixth or seventh grade, on my own, and I'd run without a bra because I thought that would make my boobs disappear. They were just so in the way. I didn't want to be flat-chested because that's what the fashion was in the 1970s. I didn't care what the fashion was, I just didn't want any boobs. It's something I've even spent money on. I had a lift, which in the end was also a reduction, even though they weren't particularly big. I have to wear two or three sports bras when I run to protect them, and it's hard to breathe with that many bras on, and in the end it's just a huge pain in my ass. They're just these things flopping around. And they don't get any better with age, that's for sure. I'm pretty sure men feel more comfortable about walking around naked because they don't have these disgusting appendages getting in the way.

I also definitely hated being tall when I was growing up. I stood out, and I didn't want to. I don't think I was the tallest person, but I didn't like being tall. Now I'm happy with it. That said, I wouldn't want to be six feet tall. That would bother me. When I see women who are over six feet, I pity them—I know it's unfair. I don't mind being six foot three with high-heeled shoes on, but I don't want to be six foot three barefoot.

And I always thought I was too fat to fit into blue jeans, so I didn't wear them until I was around thirty. I was always relatively fit—sometimes less thin, sometimes more thin—but I just didn't think I was thin enough to wear jeans, even though I was. And they were uncomfortable. When I was growing up I wanted to wear boys' jeans, not girls' jeans, and that was a big problem back then, unlike now, when they make "boys'" jeans for women.

Recently there was a picture of me on my blog where I didn't look zaftig enough, for some people's taste, and there

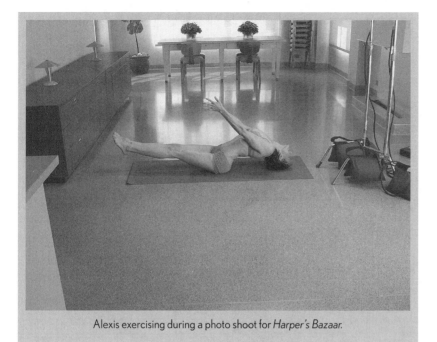

Alexis exercising during a photo shoot for *Harper's Bazaar.*

were comments like "Well, no wonder you can't get a date" or "You don't understand that men don't like women who are too muscular." Really? There are men who like all different kinds of women. There are chubby chasers. There are men who love female body builders. So how about the body that makes me happy? Does that matter to anyone?

I can't care about what men like. That's not what makes me decide what I want to do with my body. I want a healthy body and I want one that can move—and move things like furniture—so I don't have to rely on someone else. That's why I can't get a date? Last week it was because I'm a bitch; now it's because I'm not fuller figured?

In sixth or seventh grade, we were hanging out at school in the sun, and someone said to me, "You forgot to shave your toes." Not surprisingly, years of paranoia ensued. I didn't know what to do about it at the time, so I let it go for a while, but by a certain age it definitely became an "issue." Apparently hair on the feet is a sign of good circulation, so good for you if you have it, but get rid of it! Lasering the hair off your toes can last years, or for a small investment in a good pair of tweezers and a few minutes a month in the sunlight, you can get rid of every hair yourself (using a magnifying glass helps). Waxing doesn't work very well, and if your hair is dark and your skin is pale *and* you have the funds, lasering is the best option.

Sometimes I'll post a photo of myself on my blog, and people will say, "You're disgusting, and you have really big ears!" And I'm like, Are you kidding me? I know how big my ears are. I know what they look like in pictures. I picked and posted the picture myself. And if you think you're going to piss me off, it's not going to work. You can't embarrass me about that. Actually, there isn't anything on my body you can embarrass me about.

—ALEXIS

Jennifer: Make Peace with Your Body

Before I met my husband I was very modest, so if I was with a guy, we'd hook up and fool around, but I didn't parade around naked. I certainly wouldn't get undressed in front of him, and I wouldn't pee in front of him—I wasn't free with my body. My husband, when we started dating, was over all the time. We'd be having sex and sleeping together, and in the morning I would scurry into the closet and close the door to throw my clothes on.

Finally, one morning he came over to the closet and said, "Okay, It's enough already. I don't know what you're doing, I don't know why you think that I don't see you if you're in your closet getting dressed or what I see when we're together. What are you hiding, and who cares?" At that point I became a naked dancer. I was never modest again with him or with my kids or in my house. My daughter analyzes and scrutinizes me all the time now: "Ma! Why is your left boob a tiny bit bigger than your right? Ma!" It gives her an education that I'm not perfect, that her dad is adorable with perfect abs, and that none of it matters.

My stomach is all weird from having two C-sections: I bend over, and it crepes, and it's completely gross. But I have this friend—this woman is married to a plastic surgeon, she's the most beautiful thing, she's a size 0 and looks like Claire Forlani—and she's probably six or seven years older than me. One night we were having dinner at her house and she stood up and said, "Wait, I have to tuck my stomach in. I have this thing, like folds, and it crepes, and there's this skin and it's just gross and I have to tuck it in all the time." She's the littlest person on the planet, and if *she* has creeping on her belly, then who am I kidding? Everybody has something. So at some point, as long as you're healthy inside, does any of it really matter? No!

I see the same flaws with my body that I always did, but I look at them differently now. I hated everything about my body—my arms, my thighs, my boobs, my belly—but now, at forty, after having two kids, I look at my boobs and I think maybe they weren't so bad before. I've seen far worse and far better, so they don't bother me anymore. Most women I know think they have some problem with their boobs: too big, too small, too uneven, too weird. They're just boobs. They just exist. They're no worse than anybody else's.

When I was younger, I thought men wouldn't like my body because it wasn't perfect, and then they wouldn't like *me*. But guys aren't nearly as discerning as we think they are. They don't really care if you're perfect. They just care if you're

For Those of You Taking Notes at Home: Clinical Terms for Body-Related Phobias

Fear of one who has a vile odor	autodysomophobia
Fear of being dirty	automysophobia
Fear of body smells	bromidrosiphobia
Fear of ugliness	cacophobia
Fear of constipation	coprastasophobia
Fear of feces	coprophobia
Fear of dentists	dentophobia
Fear of gaining weight	obesophobia
Fear of getting wrinkles	phytiphobia

naked. And it's all how you carry yourself. It really does come from the inside out. Maybe if you're 260 pounds, the inside-out thing isn't going to really help you, but other than that kind of extreme, if you're average, it's no big deal. I spent so much time thinking my body was so horrible when it wasn't that when my body actually went out of control it was twice as difficult to deal with.

—JENNIFER

How we're raised by our parents often determines how crazy we turn out as adults. Some women whose mothers were too embarrassed to buy them their first bra become promiscuous thrill-seeking exhibitionists. Some people whose parents walk around naked and pee with the door open become obsessed with privacy. Some people whose mothers never told them to trim "down there"—or never told them much about anything else "down there"—become obsessed with "gooping." Not that this has anything to do with how Alexis and Jennifer were raised and how they turned out.

My Mother's Friend Got Me My First Bra

My mother didn't buy me a bra, and she refused to acknowledge that children have hang-ups, so nobody bought me a bra. Some friend of my mother's gave me two bras for my birthday because my mother wasn't sensitive enough to purchase bras when I needed them. So her friend took it upon herself to "rescue" me. It was embarrassing; the woman and I didn't have that kind of relationship, so it was awkward and indicative of the dysfunction in my family.

Maybe my mother had bra issues. My mother told me that her mother wouldn't buy her a bra when she needed one—she was the oldest girl—so some friends of hers gave her some bras. When my grandmother found the bras in the closet, she screamed at my mother and slapped her for having them. My mother never really needed a bra until relatively late in life, but when she was a teenager, she would have needed one, since women didn't go braless back then.

—ALEXIS

Modesty? Privacy?

I don't remember any shame about the bathroom—we had only one bathroom for most of my childhood. I don't remember that being an issue. But I do know that there came a point when it was not okay with me if my father went around naked. It became an issue. And since we lived in one of those colonials with four rooms over four rooms—it's practically like being in the same room—I remember being semidisgusted with the fact that my parents didn't take privacy or modesty seriously enough for me. My father didn't, anyway.

And then my mother always peed with the door open. I remember saying, "You know, now I have friends over! You can't do that anymore! It's gotta stop! My friends' parents don't do it! Give me a break here! I don't feel like being embarrassed! It's exhausting! I'm a kid! Stop!"

So it's funny how people change. I mean, now my mother's completely and weirdly modest. Jennifer and I went to get colonoscopies, and one day my mother whispered, "I'm going to get *that thing*." I said, "What thing? What are you talking about?" When I realized what she was talking about, I was like "Are you kidding? *That's* embarrassing?" She was never embarrassed about stuff like that before. And now it's mortifying?

—ALEXIS

Nobody Told Me I Was Supposed to Trim

I just feel better with less "down there." Or maybe that's because it's what I know now. I didn't feel bad when I was a teenager—not until the boy I was dating at twenty-two was like, "You know, you could trim." I didn't know. Nobody told me!

—JENNIFER

Just Call Me the Vagina Whisperer

People who know me know that I'm the go-to person when it comes to ovulation and getting pregnant and all things having to do with fertility. That's why they call me the Vagina Whisperer. Most women don't really understand that when you "goop," that's a good thing, because that means you're fertile and either are about to ovulate or are ovulating. Most women don't understand how their menstrual cycle actually works (which is why the rhythm method doesn't work—because they're probably counting wrong) and that women ovulate at different times, but almost everyone gets her period fourteen days after she ovulates. So that's the constant: fourteen days. Before I got married I actually took a fertility class to learn about it, because I thought it was fascinating.

I'm an expert in fertile mucus—or goop, as I call it, and as Gwyneth Paltrow's beauty and lifestyle website is called! Why she would name it after vaginal discharge I'll never understand. Gooping means you're fertile and that your egg just dropped. If you have sex before you goop, you'll have a better chance of having a girl, and if you have sex on the day you goop, you'll probably have a boy. See? They don't call me the Vagina Whisperer for nothing!

Becoming the Vagina Whisperer was very freeing for me because I finally understood myself better—I get horrible PMS, and I'm moody and heavy around ovulation. I also learned how sensitive our bodies are to stress and how a lot of women have trouble conceiving because they're so stressed out about it. The egg doesn't want to release itself into such a hostile environment.

—JENNIFER

You're Not the Only One Who Thinks Boys Should Definitely Be Circumcised

Alexis: I'm telling you, that thing bothers me to distraction. Lots of gay guys I've talked to don't mind it, some even like it, but I hate it. Cut or don't cut? Aesthetically, just do the right thing.

Jennifer: I couldn't agree more. Girls get their ears pierced; you give your kids their shots and immunizations. Just do it.

Alexis: I don't believe that circumcision hurts any more than any of the other things you have to do to children. As for "decreasing sensitivity"—I thought you wanted to last longer, boys. So parents, cut the foreskin off, and everybody's going to be happier. And waiting till you're an adult is not a good idea, because I think then it probably really *does* take a long time to get better. I mean, you're not having sex when you're a baby. So it can heal. The baby doesn't have to abstain for a year until things go back to normal. The baby has a good sixteen years ahead of him with no sex!

Alexis has always been fit; Jennifer has just gotten fit. Besides the obvious physical benefits, regular exercise improves your appearance, mood, and mental health. It also provides a perfect excuse to get out of suffering through yet another boring dinner.

Alexis on Running and Weights

I did stuff like horseback riding and sports at school, but I started running when I was about thirteen. I've always exercised. I ran a lot in high school and continued after moving to New York. Then one day I looked in this giant antique mirror I had leaning against the wall of my first apartment, and I thought, Holy crap! All this running and all I'm getting is a flat ass! (New York has hardly any hills.)

When I was about twenty-two, a friend of mine who lifted weights told me I needed to go to the gym. So I went and, thankfully, my first trainer was someone I liked. I've never stopped lifting weights since then, because I like the way it makes me feel. Do I whine during it? Sure. Every time my trainer says, "Now we're going to do this," I say no or why, and then I do it.

My least favorite exercise is bicep curls. I hate, hate, *hate* them. They hurt, in the most unpleasant and indefinable way. And they're always the last, or second to last, exercise, which I'm sure is part of the problem.

I stopped running after that girl got raped in Central Park, so then I got a Stairmaster. Stairmasters were new then. I got one in my apartment and used it for years. And then in my late twenties I started using the treadmill on an incline, and that was my thing—so I wouldn't really run, but I'd walk really fast, and I would go up to a twenty-degree incline, so I'd hike, basically, inside, and I loved that. But I can't do that anymore because of my back.

So now I do what I can on the treadmill. Three days a week I lift weights, and two days a week I practice yoga with a private instructor. This comes first for me.

It all depends on you. What do you want out of life? People tell me they're going to go out to dinner and I say I'm going running—it's the only body I've got, and there have been so many dinners when I so wished I was at home reading a book or walking on the treadmill—the food was bad and the company was bad. I don't want to waste my time.

—ALEXIS

My Day Used to Be Ruined If I Had to Exercise; Now My Day Is Ruined If I *Don't* Exercise

I do at least an hour of cardio exercise every other day: I walk seven miles if it's nice out; I do the treadmill, the elliptical, or a cardio class if the weather is bad. On the days I don't walk, I take a Bar Method class or lift weights with my trainer or take another comparable exercise class. I've had days where I have to do the treadmill for two hours—it takes me a long time to do many miles, and it's *hell*—but it's very important to maintaining weight loss. Maintaining weight loss means you have to exercise at least an hour a day. Exercise used to make me kick, cry, and scream. It brought up every emotional issue for me—truly, I would cry, unless it was a dance class. If it was running or weight lifting with a trainer, it would make me furious. I was pissed that I had to do it, because I couldn't see how it was benefiting me because I was still fat. So it just ruined my day.

But now, if I don't exercise, my day is ruined. I really need it. And it doesn't mean I wake up and I'm bouncing out the door. Absolutely not. I wake up and I'm like, Why is my friend going to be here at 6:50 a.m. to walk for two hours? I'm annoyed. But now I know if I don't do it, I'll feel far worse than if I do it. And exercise really does change your body—I don't look weird from the weight loss because I was exercising the whole time.

—JENNIFER

Weight and body issues aside, what we don't get are smelly people. Or hairy people.

Whether you're thin or fat, dealing with your body isn't about perfection. It's about basic decent cleanliness, which is extremely important. It means showering once a day. It's just not an option to go a full day without washing your crotch. Or your pits. Not an option! You have to do it whether you want to or not. We don't care how tired or depressed or lonely or miserable you are—wash your crotch!

If you're alone and you have a medical emergency, the medical people are not going to treat you really well when they pull your pants down and that odor hits them. You really better want to die. And you're going to get a yeast infection or jock itch—you're going to get *something*, and you're not going to be happy.

Girls can be so consumed with "Is my body normal? Am I normal? Am I okay? Am I weird?" Frankly, if you let yourself get smelly, you're weird. Beyond that, you're like everybody else. So at least do what you can do.

That means *bathe*. No one has to be smelly. If that's your thing, stay away from us.

And *groom*.

"That Department"

I always waxed and trimmed too much. I didn't know, either, but when the Norma Kamali bathing suit came out years ago, it was like a frontal thong—you couldn't have any hair. You had to have the "landing strip," which I hate. But if you didn't, you couldn't wear that suit.

In that department, I say do your thing. If you're not worried what your other-of-the-moment thinks, then do what you want. But deal with the consequences. If I'm going to go "down there" and some guy's got long stray hairs, I'm going to be grossed out, and I'm not going to want to go back. You don't get another chance, because it's who you are. It's really bad when you don't expect it—like when you're dating someone who's a clean-cut nice guy and then you get down there and it's as though nobody's ever paid any attention.

—ALEXIS

Alexis and Jennifer's Rules for Looking Presentable and Not Repulsing People

1. *Bathe.* We've said it before. We'll say it again. Bathe. Every day. It's the single most important—and least negotiable—item on this list.

2. *Have short, clean nails.* Don't get crazy with acrylic nails. Regular manicures and pedicures are fine.

3. *Deal with your teeth.* Perfect teeth: totally unnecessary. Nice teeth: totally necessary. It's so important to take care of your teeth; bad teeth and gums can affect your heart and your health. There are so many reasons to deal with your teeth, including the fact that not having any teeth kind of sucks. No pun intended. So take care of them. Use your floss. Brush properly—which means, up and down, not side to side.

4. *No mono-brow.* Male or female. Ever. If you have that, then the thought of what might be "down there" is totally frightening.

5. *Speaking of "down there"—less is more.* Wax. Trim. Whatever.

6. *Hide your back hair.* If no one's going to see it besides your girlfriend, then fine. But if anyone's going to see it, wear a T-shirt. Don't subject everyone else to it. It's too personal.

7. *Buy a nose-hair trimmer.* And use it.

8. *Tongue action.* Brush your tongue. Otherwise you'll get hairy black tongue. And you don't want that. Trust us. Look it up

online. You'll run to the bathroom to start brushing your tongue once you see a picture of it.

9. *Women: Take care of your facial hair.* Every woman gets facial hair. Take care of it. Wax it. Tweeze it. Laser it. Taser it. Just do it. But don't do it on the subway. We've seen that, and we don't want to have to see it again. We know it's a compulsion, but please control yourself in public!

10. *Men: Don't be primpers.* No woman wants to be with a guy who grooms more than she does. If you're a primper, better figure out a way to hide the fact that you're primping so much.

As for the plastic surgery and Botox, just remember: a little goes a long way. And a lot will make people stare at you. And not because you look good.

Duck Lips

I don't have a problem with plastic surgery or Botox as long as you don't go overboard. As long as you don't change who you are. I've done Botox, but I'm not sure I would ever get a face-lift. I had my breasts lifted and they ended up reduced a bit as well. It didn't make that much of a difference, but it's enough so I can wear a shirt without a bra.

I hate superinflated lips. They're ridiculous. They're like duck lips. The whole thing with getting plastic surgery is that you're damned if you do, damned if you don't. If you don't get it and you look old, people say, "Oh, she looks so old and wrinkly." If you get it, they say, "Oh look, she's had too much work done on her face." What it's really great for is if you're a little kid and you have a nose that's just out of control. Some big noses I think are beautiful, but sometimes it's just too much and the kid gets bullied—and I think parents have to take that into account and let their children live a normal life. If the kid wants it.

I think women overdo it because they forget that the people staring at them are staring at them because they look bad, not because they look good. People stare at them because they're horrified—either by the big duck lips or the bad eye jobs—not because they look fabulous.

—ALEXIS

9

The Devil Wore Palazzo Pants

Alexis and Jennifer on Fashion

Vagina wedgies are never okay.

Jennifer Koppelman Hutt

∽

I can't believe that not only did you Bedazzle everything you owned but that you had someone you paid to do your Bedazzling *for* you.

Alexis Stewart to Jennifer Koppelman Hutt

It's been a long time since we've read *Glamour* magazine, but we sure used to love that back page of Glamour Don'ts. Everyone's been a Glamour Don't at least once, if not a hundred times—especially between the ages of twelve and twenty-two, and especially if you were growing up in the late seventies and the eighties, when big hair, shoulder pads, and rugby shirts were all the rage. Follow us through our bad-outfit stories; feel our pain as we confess our fashion sins. Surely we're not the only ones who thought we looked cool when we actually looked like dorks!

Young Alexis in stripes and a bandanna.

Overalls and Peeing

I wore overalls for a long time, and I thought they looked good. No one else was wearing them. And then my mother started wearing them, so I had to stop. Overalls aren't fun for girls because of the peeing situation—unless the overalls are huge and you can just slip them off your shoulder. Any kind of catsuit or one-piece unit is just a horrific nightmare when it comes time to pee.

—ALEXIS

I Stopped Wearing Hats When Someone Called Me "Blossom"

I wore a hat, and on the second day of law school, I got nicknamed Blossom. So I stopped wearing hats after that. I look great in hats, but it's really hard to wear hats, because even if they look really great on you, so many people are going to say something because they never see anybody in hats. So you start to get a complete complex. I don't understand what's so crazy about wearing a hat. Why do people always have to comment? On the other hand, wearing a hat all the time can make you look like an asshole.

—JENNIFER

Jenny with a purse and an appliquéd outfit.

I Hemmed My Own School Uniform with Safety Pins

When I was in grade school, I had to wear a uniform. One of the requirements was a pleated plaid skirt, and I used to have to try to hem it and iron it myself. There are pictures of me standing and waiting for the bus with my skirt looking completely ridiculous and uneven because I had hemmed it with safety pins, and every edge went up, and it was uneven. My mother denied this until I pulled out a picture. Either she didn't notice at the time or she didn't care.

—ALEXIS

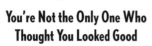

You're Not the Only One Who Thought You Looked Good

Alexis: It seems like every year there were one or two outfits that I loved to death, and were *so* ugly. And I just wore them and wore them and wore them. Freshman year in college, I had this uniform that I wore: a tank top from Brooks Brothers—not-ribbed and made from the best cotton (needless to say, they stopped making this item)—and baggy jeans, and this antique waiter's jacket in white. And then I had big bunched white socks crammed into my little Tretorn sneakers.

Jennifer: Of course you did! Okay, I can top that. There was a clothing brand called ID. And I wore their color-coordinated mix-and-match shorts and button-down short-sleeved shirts. At fifteen. I wore them to summer camp. It wasn't cool. Nor was the jumpsuit. I also wore that at fifteen. It was red.

Alexis: OMG.

Jennifer: And the jumpsuit wasn't in a forgiving material. I wore it to camp! And it was a coed camp. It didn't make me popular with the boys. It was horrible. There's no way anyone could have liked it, but I liked it and wore it a lot because it was comfortable.

Alexis: So people were your friends because you had a car?

Jennifer: Well, they certainly weren't my friends because I wore an acid-washed jeans jacket that said "Hollywood" in paint on the back covered in rhinestones! Hollywood. What a loser!

Alexis and Martha dressed up for the walk to school.

Favorite Outfits

I had my favorite outfits—and I'd come up with them myself. I was one of the people who, before anyone else did it, wore boxer shorts as actual shorts. I would sew the fly up. And I didn't wear makeup. It wasn't that I wasn't at all "feminine," I just wasn't obsessed with clothes the way kids are today. I liked my pink Danskin shorts with the matching pink Danskin tie-dyed shirt—I probably wore that way too much, but I was seven years old. I had a lot of bad outfits over the years you couldn't get me out of.

I still want to wear Jennifer's sweet sixteen dress for Halloween, but she doesn't have it anymore. I hear it was a strapless dress that came with a cape. I mean, who wears a dress with a cape to her sweet sixteen party?

—ALEXIS

Jennifer's love of Bedazzling goes *way* beyond anything we've ever heard of.

I Used to Have Someone to Bedazzle My Clothes *for* Me

I wore lots of rhinestones. And I still do. I had a Bedazzler, and back then I also had someone who would Bedazzle for me. I had tons of T-shirts from Miami that were Bedazzled. Camp Beverly Hills T-shirts that were fully rhinestoned. *Fully.* Everything—you name it, *everything*—was rhinestoned. Alexis can't believe I use the word *rhinestoned* as a verb, but if Bedazzling is a verb, then rhinestoning is a verb, too.

—JENNIFER

Jenny looking dreamy and lovely in alpaca.

Would you give up style for comfort? Or would you give up comfort for style? We think you know which way Jennifer and Alexis always go. We think you also know who totally overpacks when she travels.

Comfort First

I like to be comfortable and cozy, like when I'm watching TV. I won't wear uncomfortable shoes or clothes, because if I feel uncomfortable then it pollutes the rest of my day. I'm definitely

Jennifer with Mikhail Gorbachev at a charity event; Gorbachev and Jenny's dad were honored that night.

not a slave to fashion the way Alexis is. The older I get, the more I realize that life is short, and I want to be comfortable, and I don't feel good if I'm too dressed up. I like to be in my bed. And since I can't be in my bed at all times, I create that cozy feeling by wearing comfortable clothes. Or PJs.

—JENNIFER

Curse the Designer

I remember shoe shopping with my mother once—we were shopping for her, of course; I was probably nine—and there was a woman who was barefoot trying on shoes. Her feet were covered with blisters, and I wondered why she was doing that to herself. Why would she wear shoes that destroyed her feet? Of course, now I understand. I *will* wear the uncomfortable shoes. And I *will* curse the person who made the shoe. But if it's a hot shoe, I'll keep wearing it.

—ALEXIS

Martha Takes Everything with Her

My mother takes everything with her when she goes away, even for a weekend. Every. Thing. When she packs, she puts everything in the plastic from the dry cleaners. She thinks the plastic prevents her stuff from wrinkling, even though it doesn't. You have to edit. Think about it: two days. Just *two* days.

—ALEXIS

Young Alexis.

Don't Pack It—FedEx It!

I totally get it. I used to overpack. Until I met Alexis. When we first traveled together, she said to me, "We don't check anything. We just carry it on." And I thought, "Okay! I can do this!" I got home and started to pack, and then I thought, "Wait, this is impossible." If I was going away for four days, I thought that meant four outfits for the days, four outfits for the nights, and four alternate day outfits and four alternate night outfits in case I didn't like what I had. Then I realized it was easier to get over it, pack just the bare minimum, and move on. And it's a much better system.

Alexis insists that I point out that I also started FedExing all my extra stuff ahead of time so it's waiting for me when I arrive, which means I've actually learned nothing about "editing" my clothes and packing less.

—JENNIFER

Jenny with big brother Brian going to a cousin's engagement party.

Back to those Glamour Don'ts: here's what Alexis and Jennifer like and don't like to see when they're walking down the street, riding the subway, or sitting on the beach.

Vagina Wedgies and Bad Bras

Vagina wedgies are never okay. They're not nice to look at. It's a real problem. Not only are they not nice to look at, but they're pretty uncomfortable most of the time. So why don't women fix it? Or wear something that doesn't produce the camel-toe look? Why do they walk around looking so ridiculous? I have no answers. But I do know this: the first thing you need to do is find a pair of jeans that fit and a good bra.

A good bra is so important. A lot of women don't have one. Especially if you have boobs: start with a good bra; it'll set up the rest of what you're wearing. And the same thing with panty lines. Guys don't seem to mind panty lines, but girls do. I wear these Hanky Panky old-fashioned stretch lace thongs because they're the most comfortable underwear ever—they go up my ass, so there isn't a line, and they are high waisted. My daughter and my sister make fun of me because they're big thongs, not teeny-tiny thongs, but I love them.

—JENNIFER

Women Dress for Each Other Since Men Really Don't Care

I think we're all a little confused about who we're dressing for—and I don't know if it's possible to become unconfused. Because the guys don't really care. You could spend one-eighth of what you spend on clothes, you could wear the same thing every day—you could do a million things that would save you a fortune and a lifetime of angst—and they would never notice. Women notice. Women and gay guys. Guys only care if you're naked, in something tight, or showing lots of skin.

—ALEXIS

Young Alexis loved prints.

So That's Why Some Girls Walk Around in Tight Pants That Outline All of Their Fat

You know the girls you see wearing super-tight stretch pants that outline all nine hundred pounds of their cellulite who we think look ridiculous? Well, the guys like it. They don't tell them that maybe they should wear something else. They just say, "Come here and sit on my lap."

—ALEXIS

Overweight Women and Bathing Suits

If I'm at the beach, I really admire when an overweight woman wears a bathing suit proudly. I mean, I wasn't that overweight, and I still wouldn't wear a bathing suit. People who weigh three hundred pounds should wear bathing suits! They should live life. I admire that someone can do that—I'd be shaking like a leaf. That said, I don't get when heavy women wear two-piece bathing suits.

I don't think it's commendable when your pants are so tight that your cellulite is showing through the leggings.

One is a sign of strength; the other is a sign of bad taste. Obviously, being overweight and dressing for being overweight is a complicated issue.

—JENNIFER

Whether it's a one-piece or a two-piece, either way, there's gonna be flesh hanging out. And it's gonna be all over the place. I don't want to look at somebody's legs, either. I don't want to see any of it! I don't *really* care, but if I had a choice, that's how I feel. But the beach is one of the few places you should show your body no matter what it looks like or what anyone else thinks about it. I don't want to go to a nude beach, because then you don't know where to look, and it's annoying. That's just too much. And it has nothing to do with what shape you're in. It would make me feel awkward because I'd have to look and see or specifically and obviously not look and see, and it would be weird. So go ahead and wear a bathing suit at the beach or at the pool if you're heavy.

But wear clothes everywhere else—don't go half-naked on the subway or walking down Fifth Avenue. I've known obese people who always looked nice. I don't care if you're fat or thin, but dress appropriately.

—ALEXIS

Acrylic Nails

I feel terrible saying this, but when I was fat and I got rid of my acrylic nails, it felt good, because there's a stereotype of fat women with perfect acrylic nails. I think it makes them feel like they can control that one part of their body and appearance when they can't control other parts of their appearance.

—JENNIFER

When you spend that much time in a chair getting acrylic nails put on and then fixed every time you break one, you're not moving. You're just sitting there having someone do your god-damn nails, and you don't want to move. You want to look good even if you're overweight? Long daggerlike nails is not going to

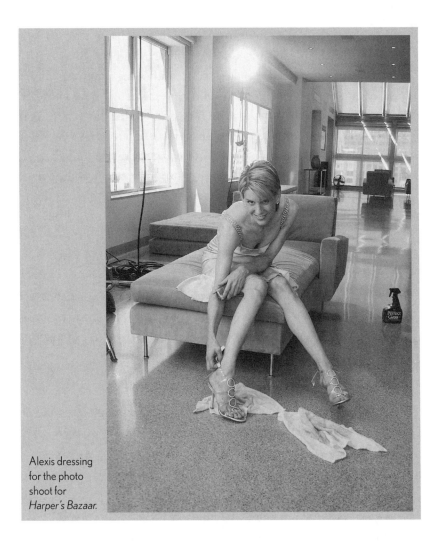

Alexis dressing
for the photo
shoot for
Harper's Bazaar.

do it. Sure, now everyone knows you don't clean the house or
do the dishes, but it doesn't hide the rest of you.

And isn't the jury still out on whether men like those talons?
I guess at least they know you won't be sticking your finger up
their ass, and lots of guys like that. Buy some pretty shoes, get
a nice normal manicure, have your hair done, and be clean and
tidy. Wear clothes that fit; they make every size now.

—ALEXIS

Whatever, Martha

Martha's never without earrings. Ever.

—ALEXIS

Honesty might be the best policy, but when it comes to "style interventions," it's certainly the most painful policy. Just ask Alexis's friends.

I Survived a Style Intervention by Alexis

Alexis said to me, "Don't wear that American Apparel crewneck sweatshirt." I'd rather be told than not be told. Having someone tell you not to wear something shouldn't be crushing—even if it's Alexis telling you.

And she's right. Crewnecks are where sexy goes to die. There are other things to wear. That said, I may not wear that American Apparel sweatshirt around Alexis because I don't want to hear the criticism, but I happily wear it elsewhere.

—JENNIFER

Jenny in her spring finery.

Friends Don't Let Friends Wear Silver Gucci Sneakers

I tell someone not to wear something only when I think it's egregious. With my friend Kevin, it's easy, because I'll let him wear the things he really likes—if someone just loves something and it's not *that* bad, I'll let it go. But sometimes he'll come walking in wearing something like silver Gucci sneakers and I'll just say, "Take them off and throw them away. Just don't wear those. You look like an asshole."

Even though Kevin definitely has a "look," his look doesn't go with those sneakers. So when things are just totally out of control, I'll say something. You just have to know what people can take. Sometimes he'll wear things he knows I don't like as long as he knows he won't see me. So it's not like he gets so upset that he's crushed—he just knows that there are some things he's not going to wear in front of me.

If you ask me what I think, I'm going to tell you. That's why sometimes I don't ask how something looks on me—there are so many times I think, Why ask anyone? There's a pretty good chance this doesn't look good, but I feel like wearing it. So I just don't ask. Or I'll look at someone and say, "Okay, you're going to lie to me right now and tell me how much you like this. Just lie and say, 'Yes, it looks fine.' And thank you."

Don't lie to me about an outfit looking good unless we have an understanding that I want you to lie to me about an outfit looking good on me. If I look at the salesperson—typically a gay guy will do this better than anybody else—and say, "I'm not really sure about this, but I want you to tell me how unbelievably fabulous I look in this dress right now! And then I'll buy it from you." And hopefully he'll say: "OMG, Ma'am—I mean, Miss, actually!—you're *so* thin and *so* beautiful and you look *so* good in that dress that honestly, if I weren't gay, I would jump your bones right now." If he does it right, I'll buy it. But if I think I look like crap and you start telling me that it fits me when it doesn't fit me, then I'm going to run out of the store screaming.

Sometimes I'll say to a friend: "I don't want the real answer to this question. Tell me that I don't look like I'm forty-five years old!" And they'll be like "OMG! You look like you're twenty-eight!" And I'm like "Awesome! Thanks!" So we can play that game.

—ALEXIS

J ust because your wardrobe malfunction doesn't happen in front of zillions of people during the halftime performance at the Super Bowl or while presenting a Grammy doesn't mean that your pants unzipping, skirt unwrapping, blouse completely unbuttoning, or blood dripping down your leg when you're walking down the street thinking you look fabulous isn't *incredibly* embarrassing.

Wardrobe Malfunction

I had these Gaultier pants—plain pencil-leg, just above the ankle, zip up the back, navy gabardine. I loved those pants. But the zipper would always fall all the way down the crack of my ass. Not pretty. Once when I was walking through a crowded restaurant with my zipper all the way down my ass-crack, a friend came up behind me and zipped it up. Now that's what friends are for!

—ALEXIS

Jenny defining the term "big hair."

My Wraparound Skirt Unraveled

When I was in second grade, I had a wraparound skirt that fell off in the lunchroom. I still, to this day, don't like wearing a wrap item—because I'm always afraid it's going to unravel.

—JENNIFER

I Thought People Were Staring at Me Because I Looked Fabulous

One time I was going out for lunch, and I put on a new pair of shoes. I loved these shoes. I put them on and I was wearing a skirt, and I just couldn't get over myself with these fabulous new shoes. But right before I left the apartment I noticed a stray hair on my leg, so I took some scissors and snipped it off. Apparently the scissors were really sharp, because rather than snip off the hair, I snipped into my flesh, but I didn't know that.

So I left my building and the doorman was staring at me, and I was thinking, I'm so hot! And then I was running to the subway and people were staring at me, and I was thinking, I'm so hot! On the subway—I'm so hot! Outside the restaurant, everybody was still staring at me, and still I was thinking, Wow, it must be the shoes! Two construction workers finally told me that I'd cut my leg, and I looked down and there was blood all over, dripping into the shoe—it was like *Psycho*. I was a ghoul! But I thought it was my hot self in my hot shoes.

—ALEXIS

My Shirt Was Wide Open

One day I went to work wearing jeans and a flowy pink button-down shirt with a tight tank top underneath. I wasn't feeling so great that day—I didn't think I was looking my best.

I parked in the garage near my office, and when I got out of the car I noticed immediately that the men who worked there were looking at me. So I straightened up, pulled my shoulders back, and swaggered into the street toward the office. I kept noticing the looks—by now, they were outright stares—and thought, I guess I was wrong and I do look great!

When I got into the building, I took the elevator up to our floor and then went into the ladies' room to pee—and when I walked into the bathroom and looked in the mirror, I noticed that my flowy pink button-down shirt was completely unbuttoned and the tank top had slipped beneath my baby pink satin bra. No wonder they were staring at me! My shirt was wide open and my whole bra was showing. Oy!

—JENNIFER

1. No vagina wedgies.

2. No pants that are so tight your cellulite shows through.

3. No panty lines.

4. Bathing suits only at the beach.

5. Don't ask someone if they like what you're wearing unless you want to hear the truth.

6. No acrylic nails. Ever.

7. All that said, dress for yourself and no one else.

Alexis and Jennifer's Fashion Rules

10

You're Only as Sick as Your Secrets

Alexis and Jennifer on Their Deepest, Darkest Personality Quirks

If you have a therapist, you're striving for perfection. Why would you go to a therapist if you weren't striving for perfection? Guess who's never been to a therapist, or only been maybe twice? Just guess. *I've* never been to a therapist. I think I've had about four visits to a therapist, but that was with a marriage counselor. I don't have time! I'm busy.

Martha Stewart

⁓

This is what a shrink or a therapist is: a *paid friend*.

Bunny Koppelman

My parents sent me to therapy for being grumpy. They should
have gone instead.

Alexis Stewart

～♪～

I'm in between therapists right now. I'm taking fish oil instead.

Jennifer Koppelman Hutt

This is like the potpourri category on *Jeopardy!* Here's
where we put everything that didn't fit in the other
sections of the book. Issues, problems, weirdnesses, phobias, obsessions, weaknesses, failures, pet peeves, guilty
pleasures, therapy—it's all in here.

Alexis grew up with Woody Allen (not literally, but watching
his movies). New Yorkers go to therapy, so to her, it's not a weird
thing at all. Despite the fact that Jennifer's mother, Bunny, used
to call shrinks and therapists "paid friends," Jennifer believes therapy's a good thing, if you feel you need it and you want to go. We
don't think you should judge anybody for going to therapy or not
going to therapy—especially if you're going to therapy because you
want to become a better person. Isn't that the whole point of therapy? To evolve, improve, grow, and change—and become less
bitchy and judgmental of other people's bad choices and annoying
behavior?

Therapy or no therapy, we don't think you have to tell every little thing about yourself unless you feel like it. Or unless you're
Alexis. She might keep secrets from her therapist, but she tends
to tell more than she should to people she's just met—partly for
shock value, because she thinks it's amusing to see their reactions,
and partly because she wants to know right away if people can't
deal with who she really is. Why waste time with people who find
you overwhelming or offensive?

We're all entitled to some private life in our heads. However, you're only as sick as your secrets. So let's get started. We're going to tell you our secrets. Or some of them, anyway.

Of Course I Don't Tell My Shrink Everything

I don't like telling my therapist the things that are really wrong, because then I'd be expected to fix them. I also can't tell my therapist anything that's too gross. Like if I had bulimia, I don't think I could talk about that. It's too ridiculous and vile. Or if I liked golden showers (giving *or* receiving). Telling my therapist about dating or when I have sex doesn't bother me, but it's the shameful stuff—anything that would make the therapist cringe (like the *kind* of sex)—that I won't talk about. Even though, of course, that's why I'm there.

—ALEXIS

Alexis the schoolgirl.

My Anxiety Is Forty Kabillion Times the Normal Level

I'm in between therapists right now, but I am Skyping with a really smart shrink because he doesn't live in New York. I have a lot of anxiety. Think of the little anxiety that you have in your

I Never Have Fun at My Parties

I never have a good time when I have people over. It's not really about me having a good time. I like making the food. I like setting it up. I like serving it. And if someone stays a little too late? I tell them that I have diarrhea and they have to go.

—ALEXIS

life and then multiply it by forty kabillion, and you pretty much have me. I try to talk myself through it. I don't take much medication (occasionally I'll take a Xanax, if I'm desperate)—not that I think there's anything wrong with medication—but taking what I deem as too much is also one of my anxieties.

Sometimes it's because you like your therapist too much and you don't want to tell him or her something you think will make you less likable. So you withhold what you really should be talking about. Maybe the thing to do is to get a new therapist and force yourself to tell the new one what you could never tell the old one.

—JENNIFER

Write It Down

You could write down your problem. Hand a note to your new therapist. Then leave. "Here. Read this. I'll be back next week."

—ALEXIS

How to Break Up with Your Therapist: Voice Mail

I've broken up with all of my therapists on their answering machines. They call back, but I don't answer the phone. Once I'm done, I'm done. It's like going to another hairdresser in the same salon—it's awkward. But finally I get to the point where I just hate them.

One recently pissed me off because I was really exhausted. We were taping the show, and seeing her took three hours—an hour to get there, an hour to talk, an hour to get home—and it was a big deal, three hours every week. So I told her that I was really tired and asked if could come every third week or something. And she said, "Well, I don't think I can keep your time slot open for you." So I thought, Okay, we're done. And she made a face when I said I was too tired to come. And I thought, Wow! A face! I don't know what that face means, but I don't like it. And now I'm never coming back.

Another shrink I just couldn't stand anymore—I think I was going three times a week, and I'd just had it. He was the kind who wouldn't talk unless I talked first, so there were plenty of sessions that went by in complete silence. I think sometimes I fell asleep. I'd think, Are you kidding? Are you really not going to talk unless I talk first?

—ALEXIS

One cornerstone of the sick secret keeper is irrational fears. Jennifer wins this category hands down.

Poopphobia

If there was a word for being afraid of everything, it would apply to me: omniphobia!

Did I just make that up, like *omnimedia,* as in Martha Stewart Omnimedia? Anyway, I didn't love tunnels—but I got over that. And I don't love bridges. I don't want to run alone because I'm so slow that if somebody attacked me, I could never get away. I wasn't as frightened when I was single. But once I had children, my mortality started to matter to me because I felt like they were relying on my being here, so my phobias got worse. My most ridiculous fear is not being able to poop anywhere besides my own bathroom. I know I should be able to poop anywhere—in bathrooms outside my house. But I can't. My body won't let go. I can't do it.

—JENNIFER

I Can Poop Anywhere

Here's the thing: if I'm in a bad mood, I can poop anywhere. If I'm angry, it's easy. It's a gift. I'm blessed. I think Jennifer should be able to, too. But as she's discussed endlessly on the radio, she's phobic. She once even had to call a friend when she was at work to go to her house and use her bathroom because she didn't want to use the bathroom at work. I mean, it's not fun to use a public bathroom because most of them are so filthy, but if you have to go, you have to go.

—ALEXIS

Flying = Death

Fear of flying is my thing. I've found it incredibly inconvenient and debilitating. And I still hate it, but once I found Xanax, I could fly. I started taking medication for flying, I dealt with the fear by becoming very spiritual (don't we all become spiritual when faced with crazy fear?) and by talking to myself the entire flight—literally.

I say things like, "It's safer to fly than to drive," "It's way more likely I'll be fine than not fine," "God hasn't brought me this far only to end it all now," "Turbulence doesn't bring a plane down"—you get the idea. I convince myself (right or wrong) that if terrorism is going to cause the plane to crash, it'll happen within the first thirty minutes of the flight, so when it doesn't, I breathe a little more easily. When I fly with my children, I have to work extra hard to control the fear or deal with the fear, because I don't want them to have it, too.

A lot of parents I know find it easier to fly with their kids because they figure if the plane goes down, they all go together. But I find that flying with them makes me feel a little worse, because I imagine horrible things and their sweet little faces gripped with fear. And then I say to myself, Stop. And I alter my thinking. My husband, Keith, booked a trip for us a few years ago and did a smart thing: he sat with the kids and I sat alone in the row in front of them. That way I could panic silently without disturbing them, and my kids got to kick my seat.

—JENNIFER

Another cornerstone of the sick secret keeper? Fear of intimacy and human emotion, in oneself and in others (spoiler alert: Alexis wins this one).

Crying or Screaming?

Unlike Alexis, I'm a total crier. Everything makes me cry. From commercials to TV shows to kids' movies. I don't care. I feel like it's better to get the emotions out. It's a release. I cry in front of people all the time, and normally it doesn't make me uncomfortable, but Alexis is a very tough person to cry around. She doesn't like anyone's display of emotion. Not even her own, it seems. I'm not saying it's a character defect—I'm just saying it's the way she is. If I'm upset about something and she's right there, it takes me out of the sadness because I know she can't handle my tears. Sometimes I'll be driving and I'll hear a song, and the waterworks just start. And then I feel better. I get it out and then I can move on. Alexis screams more than she cries—it seems to be useful for her.

—JENNIFER

I'm not a big crier. Shocking, I know. And if someone cries around me, I have to walk away. It just makes me uncomfortable. It has to do with one's upbringing. Crying doesn't really make me feel better—if I cry alone, then I just feel like whatever I cried about didn't go away. Fury will make me cry, and when I do, it makes me feel a little better. But I like screaming. I feel better after I scream.

Even though I'm not a big crier, I don't like the male rule that Martha has: that there's no crying in business. I'm just not buying that. I don't think it's wrong that people have emotions and cry over something. The reason it's "wrong" is that it makes everyone else uncomfortable. But I already make people uncomfortable, so I might as well cry if something at work pisses me off or frustrates me.

—ALEXIS

Pop Culture

Alexis: Jennifer has the most plebeian taste in pop culture. Dig to the bottom of the barrel, and there she is, smiling up at you.

Jennifer: I just like what most people like. I'm the ultimate consumer. But I like all the classics, too.

Alexis: Excuse me? Let's define *classics*.

Jennifer: I loved *Seinfeld.* I love *Saturday Night Live.* Even when it's bad. I still like to watch it. I like all the morning shows.

Alexis: *Pretty Woman* is her favorite movie. Because it teaches good values.

Jennifer: I love *Pretty Woman*! It's got great morals. I think it's important to know that even if you're a hooker you can still have a happy ending. I can't see anything that has blood or gore or violence or death or sadness.

Alexis: The more depressing and realistic, the better. Cormac McCarthy is a popular author who's depressing and realistic, and I'm not the only one reading him. But I know Jennifer has no idea who I'm talking about.

Jennifer: I don't!

I Don't Want Anyone Hugging Me

I can like you, but I don't want to touch you. I'm just not into touching. Not at all. I was kind of convinced for a while that perhaps I was never touched as a baby, but I don't think that's really true. I'm not germophobic, but I don't want you hugging me, I don't want you in my space. I will back up—way up. I don't care how you feel about it. I've had friends who I felt needed to be hugged and I've done it, but I didn't really like it—it's painful for me.

Now, if you happen to be a canine of the bulldog variety, I'll hug you all day long. Even if I'm involved with someone romantically, we can only touch occasionally. Say for two hours a day.

—ALEXIS

Alexis as
a toddler.

Please Don't Call Me

I do have a little fear of people getting so friendly that they actually might call me on the phone. That's distressing to me. The responsibility of needing to be nice to them is annoying. That doesn't sound good, does it? But it's not my fault that I'm that way. Talk to my parents.

—ALEXIS

Grudges Are Good

I hold grudges forever. I can't get rid of them. It's a real problem. My mother is too forgiving.

—ALEXIS

Knowing and admitting your flaws, limitations, age-inappropriate obsessions, and failures is a good thing. This one's a tie.

Being a Bitch

People often ask me if being a bitch comes naturally to me or if I have to work at it. I don't have to work at it at all. It's totally natural.

—ALEXIS

I Admit When I'm Wrong

I don't think it's easy for Alexis to be wrong, so she'll figure out a way to make it that she wasn't wrong. I don't mind admitting

I'm wrong—I do it all the time. I make mistakes all the time;
I'm as fallible as they come. There are plenty of times when
we argue about grammatical or pronunciation issues, and I'll
have the right answer, but she'll swear up and down that I have
it wrong when in fact she has it wrong. At the end of every
argument we have, I'm the first to say if I'm wrong. But Alexis,
she's never wrong.

I'm used to dealing with people like her, because my sister
is never, ever, *ever* wrong—not in my whole life—which is why
I'm easily adaptable and I have no problem saying I'm wrong
or letting things go.

—JENNIFER

You're Probably the Only One Who Blew Your *Annie* Audition Because You Didn't Believe in Nepotism

I was ten, and because of who my father was and everyone we
knew, I was offered a private audition in 1980 for the movie
Annie. The casting director was a friend of Barbra Streisand's,
so they were going to let me skip waiting in line for hours at
the Plaza to audition with a thousand other girls. But I didn't
want that, because I wanted to be like everybody else. I wanted
to be normal.

I was wearing a white terry-cloth tennis dress, and I was
round; I didn't look like a starving orphan, but I did have red
hair in a bowl cut that looked ridiculous. They took ten of us
girls into a room, put us in a circle, and passed the microphone
around for us to sing. I froze. I completely froze, and the experience left me so dejected that it made me never want to try
anything else in the entertainment business.

—JENNIFER

You're Not the Only One Who Never Quite Figured Out What to Do with the Rest of Your Life

I never had clear career aspirations. I had no clue. I still have no clue. I never understood that I could have a small job and that a small job could lead to something else, or maybe it wouldn't, and that would be okay, too. I never knew there were other options—other than the ones displayed by my parents, which was basically only the entrepreneurial model. You couldn't just go get a job and then make friends and then get another job and then realize you liked doing whatever it was that you were doing. I never got it. I just didn't know that you could do that.

I thought you had to be something fantastic right away. My mother would say, "How could you possibly go get a job in a shoe store?" I couldn't, because if I did that, then I wouldn't be the person I was supposed to be, because I wasn't supposed to work in a shoe store. Not that I had anything against working in a shoe store—but that wasn't what my parents thought I was supposed to be.

I don't think my parents thought much about my career. I was supposed to go to a fancy school and then do something great. After college I tried starting businesses from scratch. The only thing that really worked out was the gym I opened, because I really liked being in the gym all the time. I loved that—I like hanging out with meatheads because they're simple and tell it like it is, and then you can work out and go eat and take a nap, and it's really simple and straightforward. I don't know if it would have been satisfying in the end to stay with it, but I liked it while I was doing it.

I just didn't understand the whole thing about starting small. I was afraid to do anything, because if I did that, then

I'd be missing out on something else. But I was already missing out on nothing. I wasn't going to become a banker, with my parents' billions of dollars, like the kids I met when I went to Barnard. People always think I had a huge trust fund, but I didn't. I didn't have anything. I had just enough. I could have what my mother wanted me to have and nothing else. So I couldn't buy a crappy stereo, but I could have a $10,000 ball gown if there was a special occasion. No money, but I could have a ball gown.

So could I blame my parents for allowing me to get so fucked up? They would tell you that I was uncontrollable. But I don't think it's about control. I think it's about letting your kids know from the beginning what the real options are, what the real possibilities are, and what you might have to do to get there.

My mother went from college to being a model to working on Wall Street. What was I going to learn from that? I couldn't be a model, so now what? And I didn't get married right away. When I finally did get married, my mother was so happy—anything that was traditional, anything I did that was normal was such a blessing. It made us normal.

—ALEXIS

Young Alexis.

Voice-Over Artist

When I was twenty-five, I decided I wanted to be a voice-over artist. I wanted my voice to be the one everyone heard when they watched TV and saw a commercial for tampons, diapers, makeup, herpes medication, or any other product that required a female voice-over in its ad. I wanted to be the voice of a Disney animated character: the role of Ariel in *The Little Mermaid* was my dream gig. I wanted to be the voice of a Nickelodeon superstar (think SpongeBob).

So I made two demo tapes. One was a singing demo for animation and jingles, and one was a speaking demo for commercials. I sent out the singing demo first to people very high up in the animation music business and got a favorable response—even the legendary producer David Foster told me I had a "great voice." If you think I'm boasting, let me assure you I'm not, because even after that I still couldn't get hired. That's the industry. You're so "great" and so "talented" and so "on your way." And it's all such bullshit.

Then I sent out my speaking demo, and I got signed by a very fancy voice-over agency, which is now defunct. I remember the day I got the call that it wanted to sign me exclusively: I felt like my future was finally going to start and that I was going to get job after job after job. In one year the agency sent me on exactly four auditions. *Four* auditions! I booked none. Zero. Zilch. After that one year, I got the (expected) phone call from my agent that I was not going to have my contract renewed. The agency was dropping me—I was a loser. Okay, she didn't actually call me a loser, but the message was clear. I cried, of course, and moved on.

One week later I found out I was pregnant with my son. I rationalized that my being dropped from the agency was *bashert*, fate: I was meant to focus on my pregnancy and ready myself for motherhood. So that's what I did. I spent the next six years as a stay-at-home mom. I managed to pass the bar exam during that time, and I had a brief stint working as a lawyer a few hours a day. Mainly, though, I was home and I was happy. And even though I was happy, I still thought about the career I didn't yet have and might never have.

Just after I turned thirty-five I met Alexis, who asked me to develop and cohost the radio show. The career I now have and love was totally unexpected.

—JENNIFER

I Joined a Knitting Group and Sucked at It

I joined a knitting club, and everyone hated me so much. I was the worst knitter. This shocked Jennifer. She figured I'd be the worst club member but not the worst knitter. I was both!

—ALEXIS

When Kids Ask Hard Questions

I don't talk about my children often—I try to respect their privacy. But one morning I had a conversation with my daughter while we were driving to school. She asked me how close the cemetery, where my mom is buried, is to our house. I told her it was forty minutes away, and she was concerned it was too far. Then she asked me about my mother's cancer again.

Was it caught early or was it late stage? (Her words, not mine.)

How did she get it? Will you get it, Mommy?

Will I? How old will you be when I'm sixty-five, and will you be alive when I'm sixty-five? (She was eight at the time we had this discussion.)

Are you okay, Mommy?

I did my best to answer honestly. No, my mom's cancer was not caught early (pancreatic cancer almost never is). I don't know how she got sick, but pancreatic cancer is not contagious. I don't think I'll get it, because most people do not get pancreatic cancer, but I'll take care of myself and be tested when it's time for me to be tested (typically, a child of someone with pancreatic cancer needs to start testing ten years before the parent's age at diagnosis). You probably won't get it, honey, and hopefully when you're older, cancer will be no big deal because scientists and doctors will have found a cure by then. I'll be ninety-five when you're sixty-five, and I hope I'm still around then. And although I'm still sad, baby, I am okay.

I. Don't. Dance.

I don't dance. When I'm drunk I move a little (in bed), but not that much.

—ALEXIS

Jenny's kids, Raquel and Jacob.

She went off to school and I was left with so many lingering thoughts. It's the uncertainty of things that's hardest for me to deal with. I don't want to lie to my kids, so I say things like "I think I won't get sick, and I'd like to live a long time. I'll try to live a long time. I should be able to live a long time" and "You will more likely than not be okay." I also say, "We're all okay no matter what happens, and it's important to cherish every minute of every day and think positively and take good care of ourselves and each other." And "Don't fight! Stop fighting with your brother!" (I have to get that in any time I can!) And I know that I say "I think" and "I hope" and "It should" because I can't guarantee a damn thing. Because the fact is that nothing is certain, and that is all I really know for sure.

It drives me insane that I can't promise absolute protection, happiness, longevity, and prosperity for my kids—every parent wants to—but I can (and I do) show my children how much I love them. And I can and I do keep answering their questions, no matter how upset they may make me. I can only show by example that no matter what life throws at you, it's possible to keep a positive outlook, that it's possible and okay to laugh and cry at the same time, and that each day, uncertainty can potentially bring not just something horrible but maybe something wonderful, magical, and fantastic.

And that just as easy as it is to worry about the bad, we can hope for the good.

—JENNIFER

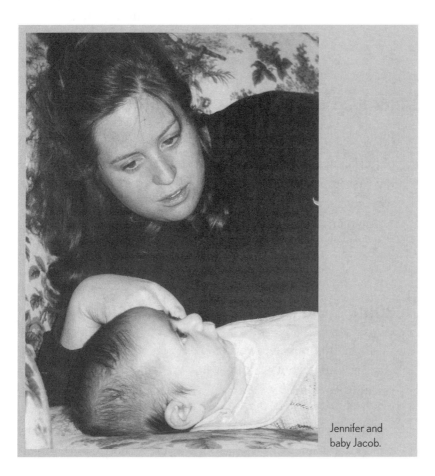

Jennifer and baby Jacob.

I'm *So* Glad Facebook Didn't Exist When I Was Young and Single

It's a good thing that there was no Facebook when I was a kid. I would have been so obsessed with being on everyone's Facebook page and having enough friends. The best part about Facebook is finding people from your past. I love that. If I'd been single in the Age of Facebook and was going out on a date with a guy, I'd be looking through every single one of his friends. I'd see which friends we had in common, and then I'd ask one of the mutual friends if I should go out with him, and that way I'd know if it was worth it to go on the date.

—JENNIFER

I Judge a Book by Its Author Photo

I don't want or need to see the photo of any author of any piece of fiction or nonfiction, because then I have trouble separating my first impression from the author's work. I also don't know why authors want their photos there. They're usually unflattering pictures, at best (check out our book jacket!).

—ALEXIS

Reading Helps You Not Sound Stupid

I asked a friend recently why my earphone buds are always tangled in a huge knot, and he said, "Well, I saw this thing about 'string theory' on the Internet." And I looked at him and said, "That's not why my earphones are always tangled." I don't understand string theory, but I know it has nothing to do with why my headphones are always tangled. I was pretty horrified. This person doesn't like to read fiction, which is okay, but even fiction teaches you a million things. *Read* something—read *anything*—and you'll learn something, and then you won't sound so stupid.

—ALEXIS

Alexis Is Impossible to Buy Gifts For

Alexis is the toughest person to get a gift for. She always says she doesn't want me to get her a gift, but sometimes people want to get a gift for her, and she makes it so difficult because she doesn't like anything except "crisp singles." She wants cash, or she'll take a gift card to a store she shops at. Even if I were to think I found the greatest thing for her and I was so thoughtful, either she'd already have it or it would be a little off, which would nullify the benefit of that gift. So it's useless. It's better to just give her cash.

—JENNIFER

I Love Saying "No, Thank You" to Gifts and Other Unsolicited Items

I love to reject things people give me. It always freaks them out. It's so subversive. "No, thank you." Who knew three little words could have such power? Try it sometime! You'll see how much fun it is to say that.

—ALEXIS

All I Want Are Useful Things

I don't mind useful things—you could have a case of toilet paper delivered to my house and I'd be pretty happy. It would have to be the right toilet paper: Scott Tissue, because that's my brand.

All that bullshit about "it's the thought that counts"? Well, that's exactly the point: don't give a gift if you don't want to think about it.

I've had boyfriends give me shoes in a size 7½—I'm a 9½. And I've said, "Um, these are the other girl's shoes!" Honestly, I didn't care—just give me some shoes in my size!

—ALEXIS

Oscar de la Renta Made Me Cry

I went to Oscar de la Renta to design a wedding dress for me, and he made a big deal of telling me how all the beading he did was done by hand and done in India and therefore it would cost a fortune. And then he told me I was too fat. I left and I cried.

—JENNIFER

Um, Mr. de la Renta?

You should have told Mr. de la Renta that if he were *really* a great designer, his beading would have been done in Paris.

—ALEXIS

Alexis and crew making sure the carpet is aligned properly.

⟋⟍

I (Still) Love Dolls

Jennifer: Maybe I was eighteen—or twenty, or twenty-five—when I bought another Cabbage Patch Kid. Maybe I was twenty-six. Or twenty-seven. Okay, I was twenty-eight when I bought myself another Cabbage Patch Kid.

Alexis: Did you play with it? Did you talk to it? OMG. You did. Let me do the equation. Loser = plays with dolls until she's twenty-eight years old.

⟋⟍

There are two ways we lose people: when they die, and when we cut them out of our lives or they cut us out of theirs. Once they're gone, they're gone for good, and we either grieve the loss of those we love or celebrate the permanent dismissal of the assholes who don't deserve our time or energy anymore. If we're very lucky, loyal, loving, and forgiving—and if we never ever try to hug them—maybe the people who remain will be our friends forever.

I Still Haven't "Gotten Over It"

Soon after my mother died, I Googled her—I Googled her!—and a picture popped up from years earlier. She was laughing, she was happy, she was healthy, and she was alive. And suddenly, she wasn't. I didn't know how to grieve or what I was supposed to do: Was I doing it wrong? Was there a right way? Why was I always crying? Why couldn't I get past it? There were days when I was filled with sadness and days when I was filled with joy, and the constant roller coaster of my feelings confused and exhausted me. One minute I'd feel like my heart was literally torn in two and I couldn't breathe; the next minute

I'd be able to laugh. And the irony of it all was that I wanted to talk to my mom about it because she was the one person in the world who would understand the range of emotions I was feeling.

She understood me—my anxiety, my insecurities (she gave some of those things to me, right?)—and I understood her, too. Even now, going on three years without her, I know just how she'd react in any situation I'm in, which is a very bittersweet thing. I can hear her voice within me, telling me how proud she was of me, how much she loved me, and how much she loved my kids. "Look at all you have, Jenny!" she'd say, and she's right. I do have so much to be happy about, to be grateful for, and to hope for. I just wish she was still here to smile with me.

Two nights before my mother died, my husband, my father, my brother, my sister, a trusted friend who is also a doctor, and I sat in the den in my parents' house, talking about my mother's fate. Everyone seemed resigned to the fact that her death was imminent—everyone, that is, except me, which is why I think we were all there: to convince me to let go of my mom. Our friend the doctor listened to my theories of how I thought we could stop the progression of her disease—listened to my non-medical nonsensical ideas for all the ways we could try to reverse what had happened to her—and then he debunked my theories one by one, lovingly, with kindness, assuring me that we'd done nothing wrong in how we'd cared for her over the course of her illness. I could pretend that after that meeting in the den I understood and I let go, but that would be a lie. I didn't let go until after she died, and I still haven't let go completely. I'm not sure I ever will. And I'm not sure I want to.

There's an odd freedom that comes with losing your mother, like when my parents would go away on vacation and leave us to take care of ourselves—the feeling that no one was checking up on us and we could stay out as late as we wanted and do what we wanted without consequences. That's the feeling I have now, sometimes. That my mother isn't checking up on me, and although this makes me incredibly sad and I miss her more than I can adequately describe, it is in fact a truth: losing your mother means losing the one who constantly monitors what you're doing and lets you know just how you should be doing it. I remember my mother used to say to me, "I'm the only one who'll tell you the truth, Jenny." And, yes, I'm well aware that it was her truth, but really, who other than your mother has a more direct and honest way of dealing with you?

In some ways, losing my mother has made me feel less accountable for my actions, and while I know this isn't exactly how I should be feeling long-term, I welcome the gift of suspending any and all judgment right now.

Now that I'm forty-one, and now that I'm motherless, I'm caring less and less about what anyone thinks about me.

The Koppelmans celebrating Bunny's sixty-fifth birthday; she passed away six months later.

Whether it's wearing a swimsuit on the beach with my ever-too-full thighs touching (I do wear a sarong, but unfortunately it's see-through), riding the ocean's waves with my son and my nephew, being friendly to strangers, hip-hop dancing with my daughter, taking Xanax to manage my fear of flying, or just about everything I do at this point—I do it because I want to. And I don't dwell on how unattractive, silly, weird, or un-uptight I may appear. For me, this is growth. And it's good.

—JENNIFER

A Dish Best Served Cold

If someone really screws with me, I never forget, and I hope that one day the opportunity will arise that I can repay the favor. I wait. I might wait a few years. Or it might never happen. I don't really think about it. Often the opportunity just presents itself. Somebody who worked for me once did a really crappy job—he was an incredibly unpleasant person, lazy, dishonest, and more—and a few years later I got a call from the police department asking me what I thought of him, because he was applying to become a police officer. So I told them.

I'll go out with some guy who I know doesn't really like me and who I don't really like either, but the sex is fun—and I'll do those things that guys do: we'll go by some really fancy restaurant that he could never afford, and I'll say, "Wow, that place is really great. I'll take you there for your birthday." It's demeaning, and he probably wants to go there, and I'm not going to take him, and we're not going to be together on his birthday. It's revenge against everyone who treats anyone like crap.

I love getting rid of friends. It's so much fun. Because usually there's a reason I'm getting rid of them. Like they've done something nasty, which means they're just going to do something nasty again. Or they're annoying, which means they're just going to be annoying again. Or they're chronically late—late to the point where every time you meet them they're forty-five minutes to an hour late. That just means they're not good friends, because they can't show up.

Everyone always says I should try to work things out, explain to people that what they do bothers me or hurts my feelings, but I don't do that. No. I say, "You know what? That's it. We're done. You're late. *Again*." And then I'm done with them. Done. Finished. Because by that time I'm so angry I don't want to be around them anymore.

If someone wants to get back in, all they can do is change their name and facial features so I can't recognize them. I don't believe in the redemption thing because I don't think people really change. I mean, maybe if they came up with a good apology or acted really sorry, *maybe*. But people typically don't do that and aren't sorry. So I get to the point where I'm done with someone, and then they keep texting. They text and they text and they text. And I never respond. I just ignore them forever. It's the only way to end it completely, and it's also a good way to punish people, because they don't like being ignored.

I know it sounds horrible and mean, but I've done it my whole life. It's a beautiful thing. It's amazing. So you better be nice to me and not annoy me.

—ALEXIS

Being There

I know I often annoy Alexis, but I'm really pretty nice to her. And contrary to popular belief, she's really been pretty nice to me, too.

The day my mother died, the worst day of my life, I called Alexis in a panic—I didn't know how to get a house ready for shivah, and in an hour she was there, going through my mom's house and helping me set it up.

She was there for me, and I am grateful.

—JENNIFER

This is the End, My Friend

By now you probably know that we're no longer doing the radio show together and have gone our separate ways. Six years is a long time for any working relationship. Things change, people grow, friendships ebb and flow—pick your cliché; they're all true. In other words, whatever. In the six years we worked together: Jennifer lost her mother and a lot of weight. Alexis moved into a new home and had a baby girl. We also wrote this book.

Our working relationship and friendship were great while they lasted.

While we may not be partners in crime and creative collaborators anymore, this book was a genuine and fruitful effort to share our thoughts, feelings, and secrets in the hopes that self-acceptance and banishing shame—two concepts that propelled us to write the book in the first place—will catch on and catch on big. Everything in here was true when we wrote it, and it's still true now even though we're no longer "a couple." While we have disagreed on almost everything over the years, on a few good things we will always be in complete agreement. The fact that change is positive is one of those things. The need to live in Whateverland—the place inside yourself where you can truly *be* yourself—is another.

—ALEXIS AND JENNIFER

Acknowledgments

I'm grateful beyond words to my family, friends, and colleagues who have helped me get to this exciting place in my life. I'm sure there are going to be more bumps ahead, but thanks to all of you. I will persevere regardless of what comes my way.

My sister, Stacy Fritz, you make my life easy. Thanks for being my best friend, my mother, and, of course, my sister, who's always helpful and who always makes me laugh. I love you! Thanks to my brother, Brian Koppelman (you're so great!). You're the best brother anyone could ever have, and I love you, too, almost as much as I love Stacy. To my mother-in-law, Sabina Hutt, I'm including you not just because I have to or because you'll brag and I'll sell more books; I actually love you, too. I'm grateful to everyone else in my family and appreciate every single one of you. To all of my friends—you know exactly who you are—the diner at noon today? We need to laugh! Thank you for taking care of me through everything. Love you all. To my friends who don't live close by, I appreciate and love you the same and wish you lived closer.

Many thanks to all of the people who made the radio show and the television shows possible, including Alexis Stewart; everyone at Martha Stewart Living Omnimedia; Sirius/XM Radio, especially Paul Kodila; and the Fine Living Network.

Thanks to Dr. Patricia Wexler and Dr. Gene Wexler, who pledged to never let me become old looking. I love you!

To my super-tolerant internist, Dr. Louis Aronne, and his wife, Jane, who have been my friends for many years. Thanks for being tolerant of my persistent nuttiness!

Special thanks also to my good friends hairstylist Sebastian Scolarici and makeup artist Berta Camal. I would look like an animal without the two of you fixing me up constantly. You two are my dream team! Alicia Ramirez and Jamie Shechtman, thanks for keeping my hair unfrizzy and never gray. And thank you to my dear friend LA hairstylist Mark Townsend for sharing his loving words about my mom.

Thanks to our agent, Shawn Coyne, our editor, Tom Miller, and everyone else at John Wiley & Sons for all of their hard work on our behalf: Kitt Allan, Laura Cusack, Mike Onorato, Jorge Amaral, Susan Olinsky, and Lisa Burstiner.

I'm especially grateful to Laura Zigman for her enormous contribution to this book. Had she not helped organize my thoughts, you wouldn't be reading any of them!

—Jenny

Resources

Alexis and Jennifer's Guide to Useful Sites and Favorite Things

Alexis's Favorites

Housewares

Awesome shelving: http://www.vitsoe.com/en/us

Modern house wares:
   http://www.okstore.la/index.php
   http://www.unicahome.com/
   http://www.lekkerhome.com/
   http://www.designpublic.com/

Cool stuff:
   http://kioskkiosk.com/
   http://www.fitzsu.com/index.php
   www.manufactum.com/

Custom cutting boards: http://www.cuttingboardcompany.com/

Cool phones: http://www.oldphones.com/servlet/StoreFront

Food

Ingredients and equipment: http://www.culinarydistrict.com/

*Great miso with great recipes, including the best recipe for the
   salad dressing you get in Japanese restaurants (I use less garlic*

and much less oil and add a Vidalia onion): http://www.south rivermiso.com/

Thai ingredients and tools: http://importfood.com/

Candy and baking ingredients:
http://www.lepicerie.com/customer/home.php
http://www.beryls.com/
http://www.pastrychef.com/
http://www.kingarthurflour.com/shop/landing.jsp

Hard to find organic ingredients: http://www.naturesflavors.com/

The best pasta and lots of other amazing stuff: http://www.formaggio kitchen.com/

More Italian ingredients:
http://www.gustiamo.com/
http://www.salumeriaitaliana.com/
http://www.ilmercatoitaliano.net

Cheese:
http://www.idealcheese.com/
http://cheesebyhand.com/

The best parmesan cheese: http://www.academiabarilla.com/

Kitchen wares:
http://www.fantes.com/index.html
http://www.jbprince.com/
http://www.bakingshop.com/equipment/index.html
http://www.bakedeco.com/

Real Jordan Almonds: http://www.confettipelino.com/site/epage/ 30439_552.htm

Candy for adults and children (a great place to visit, too!): http://www.papabubble.com/

Licorice: http://www.licoriceinternational.com/licorice/pc/Licorice-International-Home-Page-d44.htm

Packaging

Presentation is everything! No one really likes baked goods or home-made candy in a zip lock bag or crumpled tinfoil.

Boxes: http://www.bakingboxes.com/index.html

Rolls of real cellophane, plain shopping bags, and coffee bags: http://www.papermart.com

Real cellophane bags and great custom labels and coasters:
http://www.simplicity.com/p-783–3yd-of-12-seam-bindinghem-tape
.aspx

Tags: http://www.paperpresentation.com/mm5/merchant.mvc?Screen
=SFNT&Store_Code=PPN

Ribbon, boxes, bags, and tissue: http://www.nashvillewraps.com/

Ribbon: http://www.mjtrim.com/Catalog/Category/443.aspx

*The best plain white cake boxes (and a bunch of other hard-to-find
kitchen items, including the most unusual cookie cutters):*
http://www.lacuisineus.com/catalog/

Waxed tissue and tons of baking cups: http://www.fancyflours.com/site/
index.html

*Seam binding (great colors and so inexpensive; great for tying
cellophane bags):*
http://www.fabric.com
http://www.simplicity.com/p-783–3yd-of-12-seam-bindinghem-tape
.aspx

Tea canisters (for candy or cookie packaging) and other Japanese products:
http://store.zensuke.com/index.html

Beautiful ribbon, twine, and other items:
http://www.papertreyink.com/index.html

Odd but beautiful papers, labels, boxes, tags, and other items:
http://www.bellocchio.com/

Jennifer's Favorites

www.jenniferhutt.com
www.weightwatchers.com
www.solestruck.com
www.barmethod.com
www.poptarts.com
www.siwydenim.com
www.workcustomjeans.com
www. revolveclothing.com
www.cabbagepatchkids.com
www.hankypanky.com (Hanky Panky Retro Thong—not Plus Size!)

Credits

Epigraph page 7: "In 1970, while I was living in New York City," "Remembering Turkey Hill," *Martha Stewart Living*, October 2007, http://www.marthastewart.com/article/remembering-turkey-hill?page=3.

Box on page 36: "Christmas Eve at Martha's," "Martha's Christmas Memories," *Martha Stewart Living*, http://www.marthastewart.com/article/marthas-christmas-memories.

Epigraph page 51: "The Koppelman-Hutt wedding," Lois Smith Brady, *New York Times* style section, June 15, 1997.

Epigraph page 52: "I spent an afternoon with Alexis shopping for her wedding suit," *Martha Stewart Living* December 1997 as quoted in Nadine Brozan, "Chronicle," *New York Times*, December 17, 1997, http://www.nytimes.com/1997/12/17/nyregion/chronicle-647322.html.

Larry King interview, page 61: *Larry King Live*, March 17, 2004.

Larry King interview, page 123: *Larry King Live*, March 17, 2004.

Box on page 129, "Martha on Alexis," Carla Hay, "Martha Stewart Makes Herself at Home on the Hallmark Channel," Examiner.com, September, 13, 2010, http://www.examiner.com/celebrity-q-a-in-national/kristen-stewart-and-dakota-fannings-pre-new-moon-movie-with-kate-hudson-makes-tribeca-debut?render=print.

Box on page 136: "Martha on Being a Working Mother" "Discovering Everyday Good Things," Academy of Achievement interview, http://www.achievement.org/autodoc/page/ste0int-3—June 2, 1995.

Box on page 142: "Martha Remembers Christmas," "Remembering: Christmas Past," *Martha Stewart Living,* November/December 1991.

Box on page 149: "Martha on Alexis Redux," *Wall Street Journal*, December 3, 2009.

Larry King interview, page 155, *Larry King Live*, March 17, 2004.

Cookie recipe, page 162, copyright © 2009, Martha Stewart Living Omnimedia, Inc., originally published in the September 1998 issue of *Martha Stewart Living*.

Photo Credits

Personal collection of Alexis Stewart: pages 2 (top), 4, 13, 16, 18, 19, 27, 30, 58, 74, 76, 78, 81, 112, 122, 128, 147, 155, 156, 158, 160, 174, 187, 202, 204, 207, 210, 212, 221, 227, 231, 238.

Personal collection of Jennifer Koppelman Hutt: pages 2 (bottom), 3, 10, 12, 28, 55, 93, 95, 121, 124, 143, 171, 181, 203, 206, 208, 234, 235, 241.

Jenny Risher: page 6.

Fred Markus Photography, personal collection of Jennifer Koppelman Hutt: pages 205, 213, 216.

Index

Page numbers in *italics* refer to illustrations.